Targeting

ASSESSMENT

in the Primary
Classroom

Targeting

ASSESSMENT

in the Primary Classroom

**Strategies for
planning,
assessment,
pupil feedback
and target setting**

Shirley Clarke

Hodder & Stoughton

A MEMBER OF THE HODDER HEADLINE GROUP

Orders: please contact Bookpoint Ltd, 39 Milton Park, Abingdon, Oxon OX14 4TD.
Telephone: (44) 01235 400414, Fax: (44) 01235 400454. Lines are open from
9.00–6.00, Monday to Saturday, with a 24 hour message answering service.
Email address: orders@bookpoint.co.uk

British Library Cataloguing in Publication Data
A catalogue entry for this title is available from the British Library

ISBN 0 340 72531 1

First published 1998
Impression number   10   9   8   7   6
Year   2004   2003   2002   2001   2000

Typeset by Wearset, Boldon, Tyne and Wear.
Printed in Great Britain for Hodder & Stoughton Educational,
a division of Hodder Headline Plc, 338 Euston Road, London NW1 3BH
by J W Arrowsmith Ltd, Bristol.

Contents

Acknowledgements

I would like to express my thanks to the following schools who contributed to this book by allowing me to use examples of their teachers' or children's work:

Ridgeway Primary School, Croydon
Chiddingly Primary School, East Sussex
Eversley Primary School, Enfield
St Thomas of Canterbury RC Primary School, Hammersmith and Fulham
St John's Highbury Vale C of E Primary School, Islington
Stockwell Infant School, Lambeth
Whytrig Middle School, Northumberland
Bedlington Station First School, Northumberland
Parkhill Junior School, Redbridge
Rotherhithe Primary School, Southwark
Lingfield Primary School, Surrey
Halley Primary School, Tower Hamlets
Columbia Primary School, Tower Hamlets
Ben Johnson Primary School, Tower Hamlets
Brookfield House Special School, Waltham Forest
The Jenny Hammond Primary School, Waltham Forest

I would also like to thank the following people:

■ My husband, Barry Silsby, for carefully reading through the text with his usual perception, ensuring that the book will be understood by all.

■ Dorothy Grange for modestly allowing me to write about her exciting work in Northumberland.

■ The Warwickshire moderators, who, during a day working with them, inspired me to create 'The Journey of a Learning Intention'.

■ All the teachers who attended my courses 'Tracking Significant Achievement' and 'Curriculum Planning' held at the Institute of Education in Autumn 1997 and Spring 1998 from whom many of the examples sprang.

■ All the teachers in schools where I have run an INSET day on assessment, together with all the aforementioned, from whom I have learnt so much about assessment matters in the context of real life.

Shirley Clarke

Lecturer in Assessment, AGEL (Assessment, Guidance and Effective Learning), Institute of Education, University of London

Introduction

The purpose of this book

Since the National Curriculum began in 1988, assessment in the classroom has gradually evolved from cumbersome, relatively meaningless tick systems and evidence collections to a situation where we have learnt a great deal about the power of formative assessment practices in effecting and improving children's learning. We are still learning, of course. This book aims to clarify the complex picture of the different aspects of planning, teaching, assessment and record keeping strategies which together make up the main ways in which assessment comes alive. The strategies form a complete 'jigsaw' so that, when used together, a quality learning and teaching environment is created in which children and teachers together aim for high achievement.

■ This Introduction deals with purposes, principles and definitions of assessment, offers advice on agreement trialling and gives guidance for structuring an assessment policy.

■ Chapter 1 deals with the three stages of planning, highlighting important features and making links with classroom assessment.

■ Chapter 2 explores the potential for and impact of sharing learning intentions with children, moving on to pupil involvement and self-evaluation.

■ Chapter 3 discusses marking; focusing on its use as a record, as feedback to the child, manageability and implications for the Early Years.

■ Chapter 4 tackles target setting, with particular reference to pupil target setting, again focusing on manageability and greatest impact on learning.

■ Chapter 5 deals with celebrating achievement of the development of the 'whole child', valuing achievement beyond the National Curriculum, and looks at the potential of a Record of Achievement as a vehicle for this.

■ Chapter 6 takes a crisp look at other aspects of assessment: baseline assessment, value-added, benchmarking and summative testing, summarising purposes and uses.

Principles of assessment

The following list provides a starting point for what is most important about planning and assessment processes:

1   **The foundation of the assessment policy should be a clear teaching and learning policy.**
The assessment policy should begin with establishing aims and principles, establishing what the school wants assessment to mean and to do.

2   **Systems and strategies should be trialled and reviewed until aims are met.**
Once aims and principles are established, processes and systems can be trialled and discussed, modified and retrialled until the aims are fulfilled.

3   **Systems and processes should be manageable.**
Aims will never be met if processes are intrinsically unmanageable. Support needs to be given if manageability is a problem for a few teachers only, but if the majority view is of unmanageability, the strategy needs a rethink.

4   **Repetition should be avoided.**
Teachers often find themselves writing the same thing in various formats. Unless this is useful in itself, strategies should be sought for reducing the repetition (e.g. pre-printing, cutting and pasting).

5   **All assessment processes must be useful.**
They must have a positive impact on children's learning and the teacher's teaching – they must make a difference to be worthwhile.

6 **Planning should be led by learning intentions not activities.**
We should first establish what we want the children to learn, then decide the best way of enabling the learning to happen.

7 **Assessment is not one thing: it manifests itself as a wealth of different strategies and products.**
Assessment begins at the planning stage in establishing learning intentions; these are then shared with children; feedback takes place via self-evaluation, dialogue and marking; targets are set with children; assessment notes are made to inform future planning; overall progress is celebrated via a child's achievement folder.

8 **Assessment should involve children at all stages, and parents where possible.**
Assessment needs to be a two- and three-way process if the learner is to gain significantly from it. Without the child's involvement, especially, assessment is simply 'done' to the child, having little impact on the child's development.

9 **Assessment should include unexpected outcomes.**
We can be too obsessed with the 'input – output' model. Although assessment is primarily based on the extent to which learning intentions are fulfilled, we need to be aware of achievement demonstrated which falls outside our specific aims. Children do not necessarily learn what we set out for them to learn but sometimes learn other things. The source of their learning lies beyond as well as within the classroom and must be acknowledged and celebrated alongside and as part of intended learning.

10 **Assessment should include achievement beyond the National Curriculum.**
Social, physical and attitude development contributes fundamentally to academic achievement and should be given equal status, so that 'non-academic' achievement is seen as part of the continuum of academic achievement. Celebrating what is seen as 'non-academic' achievement raises self-esteem, thus increasing the chance of academic success.

11 **Monitoring should take second place to learning needs.**
Pressure of monitoring can lead to systems and formats being designed that are easy to monitor. Systems should first meet learning and teaching needs, then the question of how monitoring will take place needs to be considered.

Assessment definitions and purposes

Assessment consists of two main areas: summative and formative. This section outlines the basic ingredients of both types of assessment.

Summative assessment *(Snapshot testing which establishes what a child can do at that time)*

STRATEGY	PURPOSE
National statutory tasks and tests: externally produced, national tests taken at the end of the key stage	*To enable pupils' and schools' performances to be compared, so that standards can be identified and targets set for improvement*
National non-statutory tests: externally produced tests, to be voluntarily administered at the ends of Years 3, 4 and 5	*To provide an opportunity for schools to keep track of children's progress and teachers' expectations*
Baseline tests: LEA or commercially produced tests applied to children at entry to school, ranging from observation of children's behaviour to specific oral or activity items	*To establish the child's abilities at the beginning of their education, so that subsequent achievement can be compared and measured against actual improvement. They can also be used formatively, to identify weaknesses and strengths and provide appropriate learning experiences for individual children*
Commercially produced tests: Purchased independently by schools, these tests are controlled by publishers	*To enable schools to monitor progress through summative means at different points in the key stage*
School tests: In-house tests written by teachers, usually 'end of module' tests, used at the end of a taught unit to establish general attainment or to arrive at interim level judgements (against the statutory level descriptions)	*Schools use these to make the end of key stage levelling easier and to monitor progress between key stages*
Class tests: created by individual teachers and used in day-to-day lessons (e.g. mental number tests)	*To improve children's mental recall and establish what they have remembered or learnt so far*
End of key stage Teacher Assessment: Year 2 and Year 6 teachers decide a level for each child's attainment in the core subjects, using the criteria of the level descriptions and using their professional judgement	*To provide parallel information to parents to accompany test results*

Organising agreement trialling

End of key stage levelling based on teacher assessment has led to a great deal of agreement trialling (also known as *moderation* or *standardisation meetings*) within and between schools. Even though Teacher Assessment is no longer statutorily moderated, it can still be extremely useful to have, say, one staff meeting a term in which whole school agreement trialling takes place. The reasons for doing this are:

■ **it ensures consistency of level judgements between staff, so that all teachers share the same interpretation of levels**

■ **it puts levels into teachers' consciousness, thus providing teachers with a clearer notion of progression**

■ **it encourages a dialogue between teachers where the focus is children's achievement, often leading to key weaknesses being highlighted during discussion.**

The following model is a tried and tested, successful strategy for organising an agreement trialling session:

1 Create a two-year plan, deciding which Attainment Target will be the focus for each of the six meetings (e.g. Autumn: EN3, Spring: MA2, Summer: EN1, etc.).

2 For each meeting: in advance, ask for four volunteers to bring along all of one child's relevant work, ensuring that the four children will encompass a range of levels (e.g. for a meeting for EN3, Teacher 1 brings along all of one child's writing considered to be roughly Level 1, Teacher 2 does the same for Level 2 and so on).

3 At the meeting, split the staff into four groups and give each group one child's collection of work and copies of the relevant Attainment Target level descriptions.

4 Each group has 15 minutes to analyse their child's work and assign a 'best fit' level, using the SCAA/QCA *Exemplification of Standards* booklets for guidance. Focus on why the work/attainment can't be the level above. Record the level and the reason secretly.

5   Carousel the collections around the groups until all four have been analysed.

6   The teacher running the meeting (usually the person with the greatest subject expertise) asks each group to reveal the level for each child's attainment. Typically, three groups will say the same level and one group says either the level above or below.

7   Ask the minority group to describe their reasons for the difference and conduct a short discussion. The outcome is usually resolved relatively easily, especially if the 'official' exemplification documents are used as a check.

8   Photocopy a few key pieces of work from each collection and place them in a School Portfolio, arranged in Attainment Target order, along with the reason for the 'best fit' level. The examples below also state the next steps for children whose work is of the same standard.

N.B. With some Attainment Targets, it is necessary for the four teachers to prepare some notes for the meeting about the child, stating any evidence they have for the child achieving any of the 'ephemeral' aspects of the level description, for which there is not likely to be a product. For example, *'Joe knows addition and subtraction bonds to 20 and multiplication bonds for 2, 5 and 10 tables'*. This recording is only necessary for that child in preparation for the agreement trialling meeting, in order to enable a full analysis to take place.

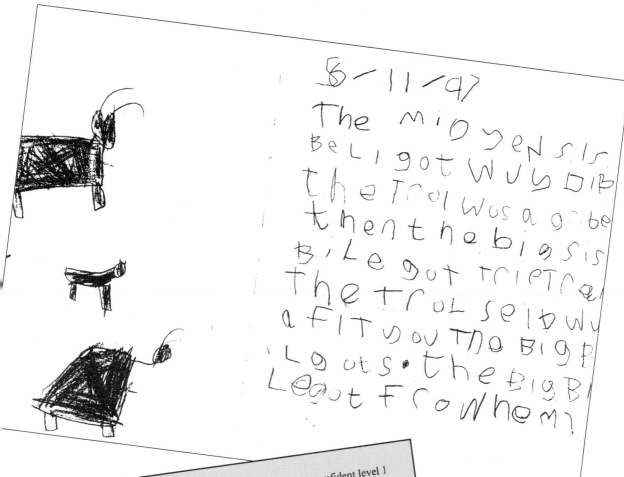

This child is working within level 1. To become a more confident level 1
the next steps are:

- spaces between words
- introduction of capital letters and full stops
- improve consistency of letter size
- continue to extend range of writing contexts

Transcription

The middle size billy goat went trip (trap). The troll was angry then the big
size billy goat (went) trip trap.
The troll said I want to fight you. The big billy goat threw him.

Examples of moderated work: Level 1 writing

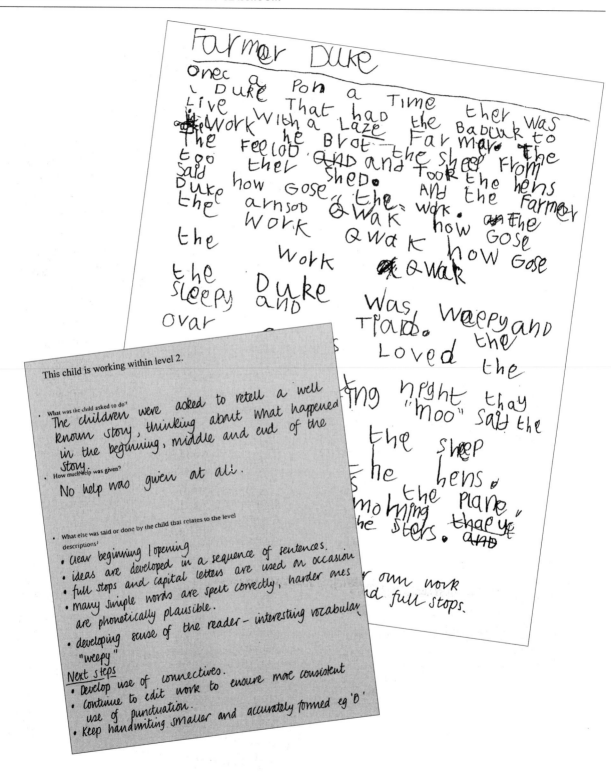

Examples of moderated work: Level 2 writing

The Day The Storm Came.

It was a fine sunny day in the middle of summer. Louisa came out into the front lawn, "Mum, dad come here, please" "What is it Louisa?" asked Nicole, her mum, "Mum can we go for a picnic today? Its such a nice day". Martin, Louisa's dad came outside. Nicole said to Martin "Martin, Louisa, here, suggested that we go out for a picnic today, and besid it's such a lovely day it would be a shame to waste at home all day". "Well see" said Martin with distant smile on his face to which To Louisa it ment a yes so she shouted "Yipee!". A hour later they were all set. They had decided to go to a park 20 miles away. On the way there it started to get dark and it started to rain very lightly. 'Oh, the picnics spoiled' moaned Louisa 'Oh, don't worry it'll soon clear up', said Nicole. A little while later Louisa piped 'Mum, Eddys fallen asleep again'. Suddenly the lightening struck and the thun thunder rolled and the rain started to rain even harder. 'Oh, the picnics spoiled for sure' moaned Louisa yet again 'Oh, stop whineing dear', Martin said. Just that moment the thunder rolled again. 'Mum I'm scared' said Louisa in a frightened tone. 'Don't be Louisa' said Nicole 'Theres nothing to be a be afraid of' she carried on. Suddenly the car skidded everyone got thrown to the right hand side of the car 'Don't worry only an ice patch, nothing to worry about' said Martin back in control and on the road. Suddenly the jerked to a stop 'Whats wrong dad?' asked Louisa scared out of her wits. 'Engines dead' he replied with a stony look on his face 'Well can't you fix it?' Nicole enquired 'Not in this weather, no.' "I'm scared, Mum" said Louisa. The car had started swaying in the wind and then Louisa started screaming. Mum and dad came running to into the bedroom.

The End

ANNOTATION SHEET
Date Monday 20th October
NC Attainment Target 3 : Writing

NC Level: 4

· What was the child asked to do?
Choose a story title – see overleaf – write an imaginative story – finish in approx. one hou

· How much help was given?
– Instructions, planning sheet available, use of
– Able to discuss ideas with teacher but no help with spelling, punct. or grammar.

· What else was said or done by the child that relates to the level descriptions?

• Spelling accurate.
• Punctuation good – including speech m marks, apostrophes, commas (sometimes makes mistakes with possessive

• words use for effect — moaned l frightened stony lo

• excellent 'sense of audience'

This child is working confidently within level 4. To achieve level 5 the next steps are:

· paragraphs
· punctuation including commas and apostrophies
· complex sentences and clauses
· extend range of writing

Writing Targets 1997-98

Autumn Term
• Organising your writing into paragraphs
• Carrying on the 'characterisation' – so that throughout the story they do things that fit in with the character you are creating

Examples of moderated work: Level 4 writing

Formative assessment *(Day-to-day ongoing assessment, based on how well children fulfil learning intentions, providing feedback and involving children in improving their learning)*

STRATEGY	PURPOSE
Planning	*Ensures clear learning intentions, differentiation and appropriate delivery of National Curriculum; short-term plans show how assessment affects next steps by the development of activities and contain assessment notes on children who need more help or more challenge*
Sharing learning intentions: with children (for every task)	*Ensures pupil is focused on the purpose of the task, encourages pupil involvement and comment on own learning; keeps teacher clear about learning intentions*
Pupil self-evaluation: children are trained to evaluate their own achievements against the learning intention (and possibly beyond), in oral or written form	*Empowers the child to realise his or her own learning needs and to have control over future targets; provides the teacher with more assessment information – the child's perspective*
Marking: must reflect learning intention of task to be useful and provide ongoing record; can be oral or written	*Tracks progress diagnostically, informs child of successes and weaknesses and provides clear targets for improvement*
Target setting: for individuals over time for ongoing aspects – e.g. reading and writing	*Ensures pupil motivation and involvement in progress; raises achievement; keeps teacher informed of individual needs; provides a full record*
Record of Achievement: vehicle for celebrating achievements of which child is proud or teacher believes are significant (refers to products and events for physical, social, attitude and conceptual achievement; does not compare children but focuses on individual progress, often unrelated to learning intentions)	*Celebrates all aspects of achievement, provides motivation and self-esteem thus enabling pupil to achieve academic success more readily; provides overall progress 'picture', although does not aim to track the National Curriculum*

The assessment policy

A policy is simply a summary of the aims and practice for a particular aspect of education. The following is a list of possible effective headings for an assessment policy with examples and explanations of what might be written:

1. **Aim/Mission Statement (one long sentence stating the main thrust of the school's beliefs) e.g.** We want assessment to . . .

2. **Principles (a set of bullet points, avoiding jargon, stating clear conditions for assessment practice – some derived from the mission statement)**

for example

> Assessment should:
>
> • be both formative and summative
> •
> •

3. **Strategies (a number of subheadings followed by short sentences explaining, in concrete terms, what happens in the school and referencing planning sheets, etc, as appendices – clear indications of practice which fulfils the principles)**

for example

	Trialling period	Date set up	Review date
Planning • The curriculum framework sets out the coverage of the National Curriculum and the Desirable Outcomes for the Early Years (see Appendix X) • • **Sharing learning intentions** • • •			

	Trialling period	Date set up	Review date
Marking • • •			
Self-evaluation • • •			
Marking and feedback • • •			
Target setting • • •			
Records of Achievement • • •			
Summative tests • • •			
Agreement trialling • • •			
Transfer of information • • •			
Reporting • • •			

N.B. To accompany the policy, it is often useful to provide a single sheet summary of the assessment strategies in use in the school, as in the following examples.

LINGFIELD PRIMARY SCHOOL
PLANNING, ASSESSMENT and RECORDING

The whole process is (necessarily) complicated. Here is a simplified version.

- Our long-term plans identify the national curriculum areas and RE we cover each term.

- Our medium-term plans show how we are going to teach the knowledge, skills and processes and include overall learning intentions in terms of knowledge, skills, competencies and attitudes.

- Our schemes of work ensure PROGRESSION (i.e. what level / complexity we will reach). [Where schemes are not available yet we use the Surrey schemes kept in the headteacher's office.]

- Our time budget (see planning policy) tells us how much time to spend on each subject.

- Our short-term plans break down our medium-term plans by identifying specific learning intentions, the activities which will accomplish these, the way the lesson will be taught (whole class, types of groupings etc) and differentiation.

- Our teacher's notebook identifies children who do not accomplish learning intentions. If a child is not noted, the LI has been accomplished.

- Our 'work completed' lists show the activities (and, therefore, the coverage) completed by each child.

- Our marking concentrates on learning intentions and sets targets for children. ('Marking' in this context does not mean just a written evaluation but can be as a result of verbal evaluation [e.g. a discussion with a child about their work].)

- Our teachers' notebooks identify small steps in children's achievement and any extra learning necessary.

- Our records of achievement note any significant achievements by the child in the areas of physical skills, social skills, attitude development, conceptual development and process skills.

- Our reading records (including home/school reading books) show progress in reading.

- Our standardised testing shows the levels we are achieving compared with other children in the country.

- Our class tests show how children are achieving in relation to their peers.

- Monitoring by the headteacher and subject co-ordinators ensures progression and high standards across the school.

- Our SEN procedures ensure that special needs children are supported and their needs assessed regularly.

- Our annual reports show coverage and assessment in all subjects and target setting in the core subjects.

An example assessment policy summary

Significant Achievement
teacher's comments,
child's view
matrix > targeting
Behaviour Cards

Identification of Learning Intentions
Sharing these with children
Day to day marking
Assessment dialogue between
teacher/child
Acknowledging child's achievements
Identifying next stage of learning
Group/whole class evaluation of work

**Short Term Planning
Book and Mark Book**
Tracking and recording of
some of the
important outcomes.
Action points. Groupings.
Matrixes/check-lists.

Fortnightly planning meeting
year group team assessment of
outcomes from one activity

Meeting between class
teacher and next year's
teacher at the end of the
school year
Transfer of formal records

Assessment

Best work samples
unaided writing
(once a term)
monitoring/evaluation of
samples (Co-ordinator
/yr.group)

**End of Key Stage 2 Tests
Teacher Assessment**
Agreement Meetings
Key Stage 2 analysis

Reports
written
verbal

Infant Records/SATs results
Records from other schools
Information to transfer
Secondary Schools

Special Needs
records

Formal Records
Reading Records
Maths Number Records
Cambridge Maths Record
Science AT 1 Records

| Formative | Key | Summative |

An example assessment policy overview (junior school)

1 Planning

Planning in the primary school consists of three basic stages: long-term, medium-term and short-term. Much of the success of day to day assessment lies in the quality of these plans. The extent to which learning intentions are explicit and focused is the single most important factor. However, manageability and flexibility are also key issues. Although planning systems should enhance learning in a variety of ways, we need to make sure that planning systems do not become more important than a dedication to children's learning needs.

> *It is children's learning that must be the subject of teachers' most energetic care and attention – not their lesson plans or schemes of work, or their rich and stimulating provision – but the learning that results from everything they do (and do not do) in schools and classrooms. The process of assessing children's learning – by looking closely at it and striving to understand it – is the only certain safeguard against children's failure, the only certain guarantee of children's progress and development.*
>
> (Drummond 1993)

Bearing this in mind, effective planning provides an essential framework within which to facilitate children's learning.

Planning in primary schools traditionally consists of long-term (permanent school documents), medium-term (termly or half-termly plans) and short-term (weekly/daily plans). The basic content and purposes of the three stages of planning are shown in the following chart:

STAGE OF PLANNING	PURPOSE	CONTENT
Long-term (curriculum framework)	Shows coverage Provides breadth and balance	Summary of subject content for each term/half-term per year group
Literacy and Numeracy frameworks	Show progression through the age range and coverage of learning intentions for each term	Set learning intentions and themes for each term
Schools schemes of work for literacy and numeracy and foundation subjects	Shows progression through the age range and provides guidance for how to teach each aspect of the frameworks and the foundation subjects	Gives examples of resources and activities against the learning intentions for each year group
Medium-term (termly or half-termly)	Provides a teaching framework for the term or half-term for all subjects	Shows clear learning intentions and an overview of activities, sometimes drawing subjects together (e.g. history and geography) Links with visits, special events and resources
Short-term	Provides a personal agenda for the week's lessons Enables certain day-to-day assessment judgements to be recorded in order to influence further planning	Should include: • a breakdown of learning intentions; • activities; • organisation/differentiation; • provision for SEN; • use of other adults; • rough time allocations; • assessment notes

Long-term plans

Commonly known as *curriculum maps* or *curriculum frameworks*, these plans show coverage only. Their purpose is to make clear to all teachers what must be taught and when. The more detailed the coverage (e.g. PoS statements either referenced or summarised), the more helpful it seems to be to the teacher, who then knows the full extent of the statutory requirements. Whenever general statements of coverage are given, it is often the case that teachers will cover more than is necessary.

Over the years of working with the National Curriculum, schools have recognised the difficulty of stating coverage for the developmental or continuous aspects of the curriculum, especially in English. Because of this, curriculum frameworks often have 'Refer to Scheme of Work' as the statement of coverage for these areas, or, more recently, 'Refer to Literacy/Numeracy Framework'.

It could be argued that with school schemes of work becoming increasingly more developed, there is no need for a curriculum framework. The long-term framework, however, is the only place where the entire coverage for a year group is shown at once, whereas schemes of work show subjects separated from one another. Seeing the subjects together means that the teacher has an overview of cross curricular links, so that planning can be efficient and, more importantly, provide meaningful contexts for learning for the children. It is also possible to track the life of a child from term to term, thinking of the terms as a continuum, ensuring that the curriculum is appropriately balanced (e.g. that some subjects or aspects are not missed out for more than two consecutive terms).

Early Years

Early years planning needs to focus on the *Desirable Outcomes on Entry to Compulsory Schooling*. Many schools have created curriculum frameworks under the headings of the *Desirable Outcomes*, so that they can be used in the same way as National Curriculum frameworks.

There always seems to be a dilemma about Reception planning; whether the curriculum framework should be based on the *Desirable Outcomes* or the National Curriculum or both, with Early Years Advisors often deciding on their own LEA strategy. All three approaches are commonly used. It seems important to keep the context of the children's learning within the Early Years framework of the *Desirable Outcomes* yet allow for links and connections with the National Curriculum, especially towards the summer term. The headings of the *Desirable Outcomes* can be used, therefore, with some of the content under these headings linking with the early content of the National Curriculum.

Reception Curriculum Framew

	AUTUMN TERM		SPRING TERM	
	Myself and all about me		Nursery Rhymes	
mathematical	Locational geometry Handling data Equivalence Cardinal number 1-5	3-D shapes length weight capacity > > > > > >	2-D shapes Time Patterns Equivalence Ordering numbers 0-5	Length Handling Data > > > > > > > > >
physical	moving ourselves > games using colours	parts of our body and prepositions,	investigating throwing and aiming	investigating jumping
	ALL YEAR - PENCIL, SCISSOR, MODELLING, SAND, WATER, BALL & CO-ORDINATION S			
language and literacy all year high frequency words & topic word banks and shared reading.	discuss & retell, listen and respond. share and enjoy enlarged texts - key characters & stories, experiment with own writing, read and write own name initial consants.	take turns in discusson(hand up), distinguish between writing and drawing, recognise printed word, write lower and upper case letters.	conventions of story retelling stories and rhymes, understand that words can be re/read, retell and recount, think about and discuss intended writing,alphabet names and sounds	perform, read, liste to & repeat by hear rhymes, recognise critical features of words - ascenders, descenders, spellin use experience of stories & rhymes fo own writing.
moral, spiritual, human and social	learning self-worth (Mums & Dads, friends and feelings) self- discipline	know about past (babies & grandparents) and Jesus/Christmas	learning self worth assembly /performance importance of relation	sequencing/use evidence & analyse information ships with family
all year listen and move to music & sing aesthetic & creative all year painting and drawing role play eg?	movement and > > > know loud/soft, action songs. emphasis on - cutting and sticking, colour home	response - internalise pulse(know when to clap after a beat). emphasis on 3-D skills, pattern. surgery/hosp	investigating and movi timbre, respect and respond to instrument emphasis on printing skills, colour. depends on most pop	ing to instruments imitate sounds,take turns, sound effect emphasis on collage skills, patte ular nursery rhym
scientific & technological	light, light/dark, shadow, mirrors/reflection, colour	growth, people and animals, Mums Dads and babies, farm visit.	materials, clothing. Familiar objects, feelie bags.	sound (see above) role play, telephone/alarms, communications.
	ALL YEAR IT, MAKING AND DESIGNING, OBSERVING AND USING TOOLS.			

Example of Reception curriculum framework

Curriculum Plan...   ...KS2; Year 6

AUTUMN	SPRING
Blocked Units	**Linked Units; "OUR BODIES"**
Sc1[all] in context of Sc3; rocks & soils [1d], solids, liquids & gases [1e], the water cycle [2d, 2e] separating materials [3a, 3b, 3c, 3d]	Sc1[all] in context of Sc2; Humans as organisms [1a, 2a, 2b, 2c, 2d, 2e, 2f, 2g, 2h]
Sc4; the Earth, Sun & Moon [4a, 4b, 4c, 4d]	Sc1[all] in context of Sc4; seeing [3d] light [3a, 3b, 3c] and vibration & sound [3e, 3f, 3g]
Geog Key Elements [1a, 1b, 1c, 1d, 2a, 2b, 2c, 3a,3b, 3c, 3d, 3, 3f] in context of thematic study; Settlements [9a, 9b, 9c]	DT [2a, 2c, 3a, 4e, 4g]
	Sex Education [school priority - see policy]
	Blocked Units
En 1, 2 &3 in context of Literature genre	
Ma1[all] in context of Ma3; shape & space [1a, 1b, 1e, 2a, 2b, 2c, 3a, 3b, 3c]	Ma1[all] in context of Ma3; measures [4a, 4b, 4c]
	Ma4; handling data [1a, 1b, 1c, 2a, 2b, 2d]
PE Games [1a, 1b, 1c] Gymnastics [2a, 2b, 2c] : Dance [3a, 3b, 3c]	PE Games [1a, 1b, 1c] Gymnastics [2a, 2b, 2c] : Dance [3a, 3b, 3c

Continuous Units

English [Speaking & Listening; Reading; Writing] (see scheme of work)

Mathematics [using & applying in context of Number] (see scheme of work)

DT [1a, 1b, 1c, 2a, 2b, 2c]; Designing [3a, 3b, 3c, 3d, 3e, 3f, 3g]; Making [4a, 4b, 4c, 4d, 4e, 4f, 4g] (see scheme of work)

IT [1a, 1b, 1c, 1d]; Communicating & handling information [2a, 2b, 2c, 2d]; Controlling, monitoring & modelling [3a, 3b, 3c, 3d]

Art [1, 2a, 2b, 2c, 3, 4a, 4b, 4c, 4d, 5a, 5b, 5c, 6]; Investigating & Making [7a, 7b, 7c, 7d, 8a, 8b, 8c, 8d, 8e, 8f]; Knowledge & understandi

Music [1a, 1b, 2a, 2b, 2c, 2d, 2e, 2f, 2g, 3a, 3b]; performing & composing [4a, 4b, 4c, 4d,5a, 5b, 5c, 5d, 5e, 5f, 5g, 5h]; Listening & Apprai

RE - Christianity / Hinduism (see scheme of work).

French (School priority) (36 hrs)

Example of Year 6 curriculum framework

ICT:
-reinforce how to look after the computers
-how to use the mouse correctly (ie: not clicking away endlessly).
-Introduce programmes to the class: in class group and follow up with pairs of children.
-learning to recognize when they have left the chosen program for the session.

E-mail/ Website:
-continue to reinforce concept of E-mail to class by sending messages and pictures to other classes in the school, and then going at specific time to those classes to see our pictures on their class computer.
-children to verbally to deliver message, adult to enter and send it.
-Introducing the nursery website on line as a display board from the nursery that tells every one what we have been doing. Explaining 'the web' as all the computers linking up through the phone line and 'holding hands'.

Alphabet program:
-continue exploring program thoroughly to children.
-basic focus of program will be letter recognition.

Dress Teddy
-naming different types of clothing
-developing 'click and drag' skills with the mouse.
-printing out 'dressed teddy' pictures.

Washing:
-Involving the children in washing the nursery towels, aprons, dolls clothes and role play clothes in the machine and drying them on the dryer.
-Involving the children in washing the dolls clothes by hand in the water tray and drying them on the small home corner dryer/ drying them outside on simple washing line hanging between the trees, using pegs.

Knowledge of the World

Exploration of different fabrics
-display table of a wide range of different fabric for the children to look at, touch and talk about.
-collage activities available for children to cut up and use fabrics (to make fabric books, fabric squares, cards, dress people puppets etc)
-class discussion times opportunity to talk about the different fabrics that everyone is wearing.

Language:

Oral:
-Making time for the children to talk about things important to them in 1:1, small and class groups.
-Introducing circle times to talk about what they are wearing, extending children's descriptive vocab.
-through role play with dressing up and dressing dolls in traditional clothes from different countries, opportunities to introduce clothes vocab in different languages.
-through puppets (in including children's handmade sock/ people puppets) to introduce and extending child's storytelling skills.
-homecorner to take on African and then Asian theme with appropriate clothes and play items.

Reading focus:
-Big Book/ Class focus on 'Handa's Surprise', 'Mrs. Mopple's Washing Line'
-Class focus on the big book text and pictures incorporating the letter of the week (J,K.L,M,N,O)
-General selection of books from 'Early reader' box.
-Non-fiction books about clothes, African cultures and Asian cultures.

Writing/ Name work:
-General experience of writing media (eg: pencils, pens, chalks, crayons etc.) and equipment (eg: different sized paper, letters, envelopes, Easter and Mothering Sunday celebration cards, forms, lists some forming part of table top workshop areas.)
-class book of Handa's surprise with children contributing their own pictures and text.
-some children making very simple versions of Mrs. Mopple's story.
-making scrap books of people wearing different types of clothes, children to dictate text (eg: pictures of babies in baby clothes, wedding pictures, sporty pictures etc)
-pencil control activities to include outline pictures to colour/ pencil play sheet son clothes theme
-handwriting patterns using pencils, pens, with sand on pictures of jumpers, hats etc.
-name writing and focus on the first letter formation.
-tracing/ copying names using namecards as well as child's own attempt on work.
-class activities on name recognition (when giving out bookbags show children's name/namecard to indicate when it's their turn to change their book etc)

Letter focus:
-Alphabet work incorporating children's names/ photos.
-Pictorial alphabet designed by nursery team and children.
-Strong connections made between children's names (first letter) and letters in focus.
-Starting at the beginning, letters to be focused on:
this half term.
-Art and craft activities to focus on letter shape.

Human & Social:

African Theme
-using 'Handa's Surprise' as a starting point to look at African batiks, textiles and prints.
-making simple dress shop in homecorner with other African type cooking things and the fruit from the story.
-children to be helped to dress up in African fabric role play clothes.
-dolls to be dressed in African print cloths and wrapped around children.
-take photos of the children dressed up,
-simple people puppets to be made using African type fabrics.
-talking about the fabrics themselves and the patterns of objects and shapes that we can see in them.

Eritrea (for Institute project)
-using pictures from Eritrean pack to look at the clothes the people are wearing, what they are doing.
-use pictures and information from parents etc to extend activities described above.
-draw into the role play the kinds of activities/ cooking/ games etc that might take place in Eritrea itself (ie: cooking over pretend fire, looking for cactus leaves, playing games with small round pebbles etc.)
-use pictures in the homecorner, as well as forming simple wall display in the nursery.
-making a simple world map/ African map highlighting where different countries are.

Asian Theme
-looking at Asian silks and Sari fabrics.
-making simple... in the homecorner with other Asian type cooking things

---

Mathematics:

Sorting/ matching
-according to colour or type, encouraging making.
-using specific maths sorting equipment
-using a variety of nursery equipment (eg furniture, zoo animals etc).
-modelling layout and structure alternati

Main colour displays:
-Blue; green; yellow (for 2 weeks each) objects for children to handle in chosen c and paper and graphics materials for chil
-a wide selection of art & craft activities t

Pattern:
-continuing with repeating patterns with through art & craft activities in printing a
-looking at and talking about patterns on
-creating our own patterns through printin
-focus on stripes, spots, checks, zigzags.

Shape:
-Table top displays of rectangles, circles, around the nursery and everyday objects
-art & craft activities to extend awareness to dot, drawing shape freehand, sand an
-shape, making shape outline in sand, pr
-badges and hats).
-introducing and extending descriptive s
-etc0 through small group and class review

Number:
-counting skills within sorting activities u
-counting buttons on clothing, fingers on
-clothes on clothes line (1 dress, 2 socks, on;
-numberline based on rhyme (1,2 buckle m
-Caribbean counting rhyme book [Helen]

Personal & Social:

Independence:(adult to guide and superv
-continue encouraging children to put the
-children to help each other to put apron afterwards.
-children to be praised when they indep and dry hands)
-whole class to be encourage to behave
-children to be praised when they make time at end of session to be introduced.

Social Skills:
-continue to encourage children to take tu things from others, to say please and that
-children to be shown how to respond se

Concentration and Attentiveness:
-children to be praised when they concen activity well.
-children who flit from one activity to an

Example of nursery framework using Desirable Outcomes

	Autumn term (first half)	Autumn term (second half)	Spring term (first half)	Spring term (second half)	Sum (fir...
First Year	Science: The solar system (PoS: Physical processes 4 a,b,c,d) 5 hours Maths: algebra, number/symbolisation ; PoS: 1a,d; 4a,b,c,d; 5 hours English: Writing: poetry, notes reports, instructions; Reading: core book activities 6 hours RE: Communities Music: Holst, dynamics. loud/soft, composition' space poems 1 hour Art: Collage: using recycled objects; elements: texture, form, shape, space, pattern, colour; artist: Kurt Schwitters 1 hour PE: Co-operative games (I); Invasion games (O) 2 hours IT: 1 hour Total: 21 hours This leaves average 30 minutes a week unallocated - could go towards Planetarium visit	Geography: contrasting UK locality (two parallel topics, one to include residential component) settlement, places. 4 hours Maths: Direction, position, angles, co-ordinates, size and scale, maps and plans, number/addition and subtraction, PoS: 1a; 2d; 3b; 5 hours English: Writing: story, notes, letters; Reading: core book activities 6 hours RE: Communities Te: We can travel (1abc,2abc,3abcdefg, 4abcdefg,5abcdefhijk) 1.5 hours Music: Pitch, environment noises, composition 1 hour Art: Drawing, painting, 3D: images from environment; elements: line, shape, space, colour, tone; Artist (female) 1 hour PE: Orienteering (O); Gymnastics (symmetry)(I) 2 hours IT: 1 hour Total 21.5 hours	Geography: Rivers of the world 4 hours Language and creative arts focus on cultures based on rivers. 1.5 hours Maths: length, area, temperature, number/ordering; PoS:2a; 1c; 5 hours English: Writing: story, notes, reports, instructions; Reading: core book activities 6 hours RE: What is a Muslim? Music: notations, rhythm, composition, river/sea songs 1 hour Art: Painting, drawing, printing - water; elements: line, tone, shape, space, colour; artist: David Hockney 1 hour PE: Invasion games (O); trad. dance (I) 2 hours IT: 1 hour Total: 21.5 hours	Science: Materials (PoS: Materials and their properties 1 a,b,c, 2a,b,c, 3a,b) 4 hours Maths: Volume, capacity, weight, number/estimation; PoS:1a,d; 5 hours English: Writing: Notes, reports, instructions, poetry; Reading: core book activities 6 hours RE: What is a Muslim? Te: Clothes/inventors - resistive (1abc,2abc, 3abcdefg,4abcdefg,5abcdefghjk) 1.5 hours Music timbre, composition, 'myself' songs 1 hour Art: Textiles; artist (female) 1 hour PE: striking/fielding games (O); gymnastics (trans. body weight) (I) 2 hours IT: 1 hour Total: 21.5 hours	Science: Processes Maths: d number/r English: posters; R RE: Wha Music: tex Art: Pain habitats; artist: Ro PE: ov IT: This leav unalloca
Second Year	Science: ourselves (PoS: Life and Living Processes 2 a,b,f) 3.5 hours Maths: volume, capacity, weight, number/rounding off ; PoS: 1a; 2a: 5 hours English: Writing: story, notes and posters; Reading: core book activities 6 hours RE: The Bible Te: Food is fun. All of us - food (1ab.2abc. 3abcdefg. 4abcdefg. 5abfghijk) 2 hours Music: Tempo, composition 1 hour Art: 3D, drawing, printing - mosaics, Celtic patterns; elements: all; artists: ancient (museum visit) 1 hour PE: co-operative games (I); invasion games	History: Romans, Anglo Saxons and Vikings in Britain (PoS: In depth study is Vikings) 4 hours Maths: algebra, number/approximation, division and multiplication; PoS: 1b,d; 4a,b,c,d: 5 hours English: Writing: story, notes, explanations Reading: core book activities 6 hours RE: The Bible Music: composition, structure 1 hour Art: Drawing, textiles, (weaving) - landscapes; elements: line, tone, pattern, texute, shape, space; artist: Laura Knight 1 hour PE: orienteering (O), gymnastics	Science: circuits and electricity (PoS: Physical Processes 1 a,b) 3.5 hours, Maths: length, area, 2D and 3D shapes, number/symbolisation, addition and subtraction; PoS: 1a,b; 3a 5 hours English: Writing:Poetry, notes, reports, posters; Reading: core book activities 6 hours RE: The Qur'an Te: Indoors/outdoors - resistive/textile (1abc,2abc,3abcdefg,4abcdefg,5abcdefjk) 2 hours Music: dynamics, composition 1 hour Art: Printing, collage - 1960's art; elements: colour, pattern, tone, space; artist	History: Britain since 1930 (focus on 1960's although focus can change) 4 hours Maths: data handling, probability, number/place value, ordering; Pos: 1a: 3a,b,c; 2b; 5 hours English: Writing: diaries, notes. explanations; Reading: core book activities 6 hours RE: The Qur'an Music: singing (Beatles, Bowie, 'World music'), pitch, composition 1 hour Art: drawing, textiles (applique, embroidery) - shape; elements: shape, clobur, line, pattern; artist: Kaudinsky 1 hour	Science: Processe Maths: symmet English: explan RE: Sp Te: Ke (1abc,2a IT: Music: compo

Example of mixed-age curriculum framework: Years 3 and 4

Coverage of the Foundation Subjects since September 1998

In order to focus adequately on literacy and numeracy, schools now have, temporarily, considerable freedom in the way they cover the foundation subjects. Apart from ICT (Information Communication Technology) and Religious Education, primary schools have been given a set of guidelines describing how they might redesign their curriculum framework.

Although the National Curriculum was viewed by many as

overburdened, this radical change has caused a number of concerns. A strength of the previous model was that it provided a basic entitlement of a broad curriculum for all children regardless of the school they attended (consistency in the quality of coverage was not of course ensured). That entitlement is at the heart of the issues concerning changes to the curriculum.

Some strategies for covering the foundation subjects

A clear option is to leave the school's curriculum framework as it is. It is not statutory to reduce the foundation subjects; it is simply an opportunity to do so. It seems sensible, therefore, to make changes only to those subjects which appear to dominate the curriculum or which teachers find unwieldy. Of course, subject coordinators might feel strongly about aspects of their subjects and there is a great danger that aspects of a subject which are *difficult to teach* are marginalised, when they might be crucial to children's learning. Subjects which schools feel they have developed and managed appropriately would probably be best left alone, as long as there is still time to fulfil the numeracy and literacy demands. The QCA 'bare bones' advice (stating the aspects of each subject which are fundamental to its teaching) will be seen by many schools as a helpful framework for replotting some of the subjects. If most schools were to use this advice, it would ensure some kind of consistency between schools.

Problems of balance might arise if schools chose to delete whole themes from the curriculum. Reducing the number of history study units, for example, might mean that children do not encounter history for several terms. The basic dilemma here seems to be between reducing the content to 'little and often' or simply axing various aspects altogether. With the first the curriculum is more balanced but still crowded and with the second there is less balance but a greater opportunity to cover the curriculum in more depth, therefore proving more meaningful learning contexts.

Another danger might be to establish new themes without clear learning intentions, leading to an activity-led curriculum. If schools choose to create new aspects of the foundation subjects, it will be important to create learning intentions (school-based 'Programmes of Study') for them, so that learning aims are clear.

As with any policy, it is essential to begin with a set of aims and principles. Once these have been determined, strategies need to be explored which enable the aims and principles to be fulfilled. The approach less likely to succeed is to ask *'What are we supposed to do?'* Consider the QCA advice, look at your teaching and learning policy, establish your own rationale and aims, then set out to fulfil them in the way which seems most professionally and educationally viable.

Schemes of work (part of the long-term stage)

Schemes of work are written for each subject of the National Curriculum, and primarily show progression throughout the school for each subject. Commonly, learning intentions are listed for each year of the school, then various columns show links with activities and resources. Despite the wide range of ability in most classes, the learning intentions listed for English and mathematics, especially, indicate the expectation for the *average* child in the class. This provides an important pitch for teaching, with the assumption that differentiation would be achieved at the short-term planning stage, or by looking at adjacent year group learning intentions within the scheme of work for those children at the extreme ends of the differentiation range. The teacher uses the schemes of work to create the medium-term plan. The following examples of pages from schemes of work show how different the needs of each subject are in how the scheme needs to be formatted. With suggested schemes of work now being provided by QCA, much of the work previously done by schools will be eliminated. However, the QCA schemes may well need to be modified according to the needs of the school and the teachers' professional judgement.

The link between schemes of work and medium-term plans

For the 'blocked' aspects of the National Curriculum (e.g. history, geography or science units) it has become quite common for the medium-term planning sheet to be passed

DRAFT ENGLISH SCHEME OF WORK

READING READING READING READING READING READING READING READING READING READING READING READING READING

Key Stage 1: Y1

key text	key author	poetry	key poet	plays	fiction genre
Emma's Suprise Birthday Outing	**Pat Hutchins** Don't forget the bacon Goodnight Owl Rosie's Walk The Wind Blew Little Pink Pig (lots of other titles in school) **Jill Murphy** All in one piece Five minutes peace On the way home A piece of cake	Catkins poetry readers More Catkins sets of 10 different books Anthology: Purple Paintbox (Blue and Green in school) Dabbling Free: anthology in group set plus teacher's notes	**Alan Ahlberg** in school: Heard it in the playground The mighty Slide *Please, Mrs Butler*	Take part titles in group sets	longer picture series families

Key Stage 1: Y2

key text	key author	poetry	key poet	plays	fiction genre
Horse Pie group set and tape	**Dick King-Smith** The guard dog Connie and Rollo George Speaks Omnibombulator Happy Mouseday Horace and Maurice **Anthony Browne** I like books The tunnel Willy and Hugh Willy the Champ Willy the Wimp	Conkers poetry readers sets of 10 books More Conkers poetry sets of 10 books Jill Bennett: anthologies: Tasty Noisy Playtime People Machine	**A.A. Milne** Now we are six When we were very young	Take part titles in group sets Meg and Mog: four plays	humour short novel interpretation of illustrations beyond literal

Key stage 1: excerpt from reading scheme of work

Physical Processes

Programmes of study	Year 3	Year 4	Year 5	Year 6
1a a complete circuit, including a battery or power supply, is needed to make electrical devices work	Simple circuits		Revise need for complete circuit	
1b switches can be used to control electrical devices	Making own switch with balsa, a paper clip and drawing pins		Making switch with corriflute, paper clip and split pins	
1c ways of varying the current to make bulbs brighter or dimmer	Effect of placing different number of bulbs in series		Revise placing various numbers of bulbs in series. Also try different voltage bulbs in a circuit. Effect of using parallel circuits.	
1d making and following series circuit drawings and diagrams	Circuits made using pictures of components except battery-where a simple symbol will be used		Circuit digrams completed in symbols. Make circuits following given diagrams.	
2a there are forces of attraction and repulsion between magnets, and forces of attraction between magnets and other materials	Magnets attract objects made of iron and steel. Dangling magnets-to see forces of attraction and repulsion. Design own magnetic games Looking after magnets.		Revise which materials are attracted by magnets. Different magnets have different strengths and this is not dependent on size. Behaviour of floating ring magnets to show repulsion. Magnets can work through some materials. Lines of force around a magnet-iron filings. Making a compass.	
2b objects have weight-gravitational attraction between them and the Earth	Gravity is the name of the force that pulls objects to the surface of the Earth.		Show the force of gravity using an arrow pointing downwards in diagrams	
2c friction, and air resistance, as a force which slows moving objects	Making parachutes which fall safely-does string length, shape of the canopy or weight have any effect? Egyptian rollers to help move heavy object-reducing friction		Gyrocopters and freefallers- diagrams of the forces acting on these in flight. Friction-force needed to move an object over different surfaces. Pros and cons of friction.	
2d when springs and elastic bands are stretched they exert a force on whatever is stretching them		Stretch paper springs of different shapes using paper clips as weights. How many will they hold before breaking.		Find examples where springs are used to keep things either closed or together. E.g. a pinball game, a firedoor and the spring in a stapler.
2e when springs are compressed they exert a force on whatever is compressing them		Pop- up cards with paper springs		Combined with DT work on mechanisms study simple toys like jack-in-the-box or the trigger in a toy gun. Links with discussion of a 'reaction force'. Is a crazy spring, the kind that climbs stairs, a real 'spring' or do we just call it one because it looks like one?
2f forces act in particular directions	Showing direction of push or pull	Using diagrams with arrows to show the different forces acting in various situations		

Key Stage 2: excerpt from science scheme of work

Design and Technology   KEY STAGE 2 PLANNING SHEET

KEY STAGE 2	MATERIALS								KNOWLEDGE AND UNDERSTANDING				
UNITS OF WORK	stiff and flexible sheet materials	framework materials	mouldable materials	textiles	food	mechanical components	electrical components	construction kits	materials & components- how working characteristics relate to use	combining/mixing materials to create more useful properties	mechanisms	electrical circuits	structures
Year 5													
Air raid shelter	*									*			*
Motorised vehicle	*	*				*	*	*	*	*	*	*	*
Design a gas mask									*	*			
Purse/belt				*					*	*			*
Year 6													
Mechanic -	*	*				*			*	*	*		
Pneumatics	*		*	*		*		*	*	*	*		*
Greek day					*					*			
Salt dough			*							*			

Key Stage 2: excerpt from design and technology scheme of work

Design and Technology   KEY STAGE 2 PLANNING SHEET

DESIGNING SKILLS							MAKING SKILLS						
3a: use information sources in their designing	3b: generate ideas, considering the users and purposes	3c: clarify ideas, develop criteria and suggest ways forward	3d: consider appearance, function, reliability	3e: communicate & model ideas	3f: develop a planned sequence and suggest alternatives	3g: evaluate design ideas against user & purpose and suggest ways forward	4a: select appropriate tools, materials and techniques	4b: measure, mark out, cut and shape	4c: join and combine materials and components	4d: apply additional finishing techniques	4e: select and plan use of materials, equipment and processes	4f: evaluate and test their product.	4g: implement improvements they have identified
*	*		*		*	*	*	*	*	*	*	*	
		*	*	*			*	*	*	*		*	*
*	*	*	*			*							
*	*	*	*		*	*	*	*	*	*	*	*	*
*	*	*	*	*	*	*	*	*	*	*	*	*	*
*	*	*	*	*	*	*		*	*	*	*	*	
*	*								*		*	*	
*	*	*			*		*	*	*	*	*		

on in printed form to the teacher teaching that year group in the following year, thus becoming both a medium-term plan and a scheme of work. This has occurred because, in the cases where the same teacher took the class, it seemed pointless to write out the same plans again.

Some schools prefer this approach, changing the activities if they want to, but at least having a starting point. Others prefer to use the subject scheme of work as a document from which they plan onto the medium-term plan, again choosing from the suggested activities. There is little difference between the two approaches, except that the latter perhaps means that the teacher will not feel so duty bound to follow the activities as in the first approach, where they are already on the plan and the former is more manageable. Some people argue that writing the medium-term plan afresh every term means having to copy out much from the scheme of work or last year's plan, whereas others say that they would prefer to contextualise the activities in their own way.

The most important things to consider here are whether the systems you use fulfil your aims for planning and teaching. Do they help you provide an overview of good activities which you and the children will be interested in? Is the system manageable? Is repetition writing avoided where possible to save teachers' valuable time? If a new teacher has to take on last year's medium-term plans, will she be able to understand what the previous teacher meant? Can we assume that every activity is the best way of contextualising the learning intentions? This last question is critical. For manageability reasons, teaching of the National Curriculum has become extremely structured. One of the strengths of British education has always been our creative approach to education, striving for meaningful contexts for children's learning. It is still possible to maintain that reputation, if we create an environment in which teachers can plan for coverage of the learning intentions according to their own ideas and inspiration as well as with the support of school schemes of work and previous plans.

Different ways of contextualising the same coverage

Teaching for coverage of the Victorian era, for instance, could be contextualised by different teachers in completely different ways, yet each will still cover the requirements of the National Curriculum. The following section lists a number of ways in which a unit of work can be contextualised. Different aspects of the National Curriculum or the *Desirable Outcomes* lend themselves to different contexts.

1   **A character**
*The topic is called: **Betty Smith 1885** (she is an invented 14-year-old parlour maid working in service in the nearest Victorian street to the school – all our work will focus on her life, her surroundings, her family, etc).*

2   **A building**
*Because our school is Victorian, the topic is called _____ **School 1890** (all our work focuses on the people in the school, the surroundings, the transport around it, etc).*

3   **An event**
*The topic is called **'The Great Exhibition'** (all our work focuses on the content of the exhibition and the relevance of all the exhibits, covering our school history requirements).*

4   **A story**
*The topic is given **the title of a novel** which I have selected. (It must be something about a Victorian family or child which I can read to the children to begin the work, then all subsequent activities will be derived from incidents in the book).*

Further context possibilities for other areas of the curriculum

5   **A role play area**
*A role play area is set up in the classroom (e.g. **a fruit and veg shop** or a hospital) which forms the focus for our work on, say, health or the body.*

6   **A key question**
All our work is focused on trying to answer a question (e.g. Why don't we fall off the earth? or How does an aeroplane stay up in the air?)

Numeracy and Literacy

With the advent of the Numeracy and Literacy projects, much of the demand for a school scheme of work for these subjects appears to have diminished. However, this is certainly not the case. Both projects prescribe what will be taught, when it will be taught and give a basic framework for lessons. However, the context and actual activities are not specified, although suggestions are made in places. It is more necessary than ever, therefore, to provide teachers with appropriate ideas for contextualising the coverage in the form of good ideas, activities and references to resources. The learning intentions column of the mathematics or English scheme of work, however, will probably be more useful to teachers if it mirrors those listed in the Numeracy and Literacy frameworks rather than the Programmes of Study, which are likely to continue to contain more general statements.

Medium-term plans

The medium-term plan is usually written for a term or half-term and provides a framework for teaching over that time.

Making learning intentions explicit

It is at this stage (or, ideally, at the scheme of work stage) that learning intentions need to be made as clear as possible, for three reasons: firstly, so that the corresponding activity links closely to its aim; secondly, so that the teacher knows exactly why children are involved in an activity and is then in a position to more easily share the learning intention with them; and thirdly, to ensure that learning intentions follow a progression throughout the school and are not so general as to encourage repetition. The importance of sharing learning intentions with children is dealt with in some depth in Chapter 2.

In order to make learning intentions explicit, it is necessary to go through several stages. The starting point is the Programmes of Study statement, which hopefully will have been broken down in the scheme of work if it is too general. The statement then needs to begin in a way which shows what kind of learning intention it is. The following beginnings are most commonly used:

- **to know** . . . (*knowledge:* factual information, e.g. names, dates, labels, events)

- **to be able to** . . . (*skills:* using knowledge, using resources covered in the Programmes of Study)

- **to understand** . . . (*concepts:* understanding reasons, causes and effects, how things work, etc.)

- **to be aware of** . . . (*attitude:* empathy, awareness of the environment, etc).

'Map reading skills', for example, is not a learning intention as it does not say whether the map reading skills are to take the form of information, ability to use, understanding or even awareness of their existence! *'To be able to use map reading skills'* slightly improves the learning intention, because we now know this is a skill. It then needs to be considered whether the learning intention needs further breaking down: which aspects of map reading? *'To be able to use map reading skills of using the key and reading map co-ordinates'* gives a complete learning intention, providing maximum information about what is to be learnt, thus making the task of deciding activities easier.

Learning intentions with 'fuzzy' words can be made clearer by inserting bracketed examples, as follows:

'To be able to identify (e.g. orally or written) geographical features (e.g. canal, hills, buildings, landmarks, roads) in the local area.'

The 1997 SCAA publication *Teacher Assessment in Key Stage 2* gives a number of examples of explicit learning intentions, which would be very useful to share with teachers. Although their context is Key Stage 2 coverage, the ways in which the intentions have been broken down can be applied to all phases of primary education.

It might seem a daunting task to spend so long on every learning intention, but this time will be an investment. Many schools are now spending time getting the learning intentions in medium-term plans and/or schemes of work as explicit as possible, first using teachers' existing plans as a starting point, then using subject co-ordinators or teams to improve the learning intentions still further, so that future medium-term planning sheets can be presented to teachers *with the learning intention column pre-printed*. While it is important to keep the 'Activities' column flexible, it seems profitable to establish the learning intentions, so that consistency is applied for what is to be learnt. The learning intentions at the medium-term stage are intended for whole class use, so they still have the flexibility to be broken down and reinterpreted for differentiation purposes at the short-term stage. It seems sensible, wherever possible, to pre-print information which teachers currently have to copy out every year or recreate when there is nothing to be gained by allowing flexibility.

Using the plan effectively

It is often more useful to describe activities in the medium-term plan *in general terms*, so that, at the short-term stage, the activities can be made as long or as short as the teacher feels is necessary, depending on how well the children appear to be understanding the related concepts so far. Detailed notes for activities, including differentiation, are more commonly found in short-term plans only.

Instead of writing an activity to correspond with each learning intention, a better approach seems to *aim for as few activities as possible*, each containing a number of learning intentions over time, so that longer, more meaningful tasks take place, which enable learning to go into more depth. For example, an activity *'To find out as much as possible about Queen Victoria'*, will cover a number of learning intentions if organised over several sessions. With the appropriate range of information texts of different reading levels, differentiation could focus children on different aspects (e.g. from finding out some simple facts about her life to finding out as much as possible about what happened in her life in a significant year, with various stages in between). This might cover information retrieval skills, involve time lines, understanding the importance of key characters and events, as well as literacy skills and possibly art techniques.

When the pressure is high, it is common for the 'Activities' column of a medium-term plan to be the first point of reference when deciding what should go on the short-term plan. This can lead to an activity-led curriculum, where the curriculum consists mainly of trying to cover all the activities created. Perhaps a better approach is to *go to the*

Medium Term Plan (block)

Year Group: 3/4	Term: Spring 1st half	Year of Cycle: 2	Topic/context: Decade of the Beatles	Time: Hi: 24 Mu: 10.5 Ar: 10.5

Learning Intentions	Suggested activities	Special Resources/visits	Evaluation (info. useful for next person doing topic)
To know dates of WWII	Class timeline; counting in tens and rounding off - which is nearest; watch video (note taking)	Video: How we used to live; Domestic Blitz; Beatles story	
To know how WWII changed people's lives	Job surveys (jobs in the home - who does what);making charts of men's/women's jobs before/after war (inc data handling/IT)		
To know when the depression was and what it was like to live then.	Pogs; timeline; drama	Music: tapes of Beatles songs; words/music of songs to be learnt; 1940.s/50's music; African music; drama tape(moonwalk); Bob Dylan/protest songs to be listened to/learnt; David Bowie song	
To understand how 50's music made young people feel.	Play music and dance; talk about feelings/rebellion; compare music listened to by adults at the time		
To know the names of the Beatles, where they came from an, when they became famous and to know some of their songs.	Learn songs; add to timeline; make Beatles timeline; make info book about them ('jigsaw'); watch video (note taking)	Books: When the wind blows (if appropriate); Beatles anthology; PDC loan	
To know some of the other important events that happened during the 1960's e.g. moon landing, Nelson Mandela, world cup, assassination of Kennedy	Drama and drama (diary) writing; David Bowie song; art	Artefacts: e.g singles, albums, photos; info/pics on war years e.g jobs for men/women; PDC suitcase if suitable; old newspaper reports (PDC?)	
To be aware that there were lots of new inventions and how this changed people's lives e.g. record players, TV, advertising, gadgets in the home	Designing/looking at advertisements; comparing 60's/90's home; 'disass(?) gadgets (IT); writing explanatio		
To understand how people felt about the 1966 world cup.	Put events on timeline; finding info from e.g newspaper reports; writing headlines		
To be aware how the nuclear bomb made many people protest.	Story (?)		

NC block areas: Art, History, Music ——— Please attach copy o

Medium-term plans: example of Year 3–4 half-termly plan

LEARNING INTENTIONS	ACTIVITIES
Science (Materials) **Topic-Pattern, Shape, Structure.**	Assessment of children's understanding of materials .Individual work. What materials do you need to build a house ?
Concept : • understanding that different materials are used for different purposes and these uses are related to their properties .	Year 1 : collection of materials discussion of them in terms of colour , shape and texture (wood , glass stone, rubber, brick, metal ,plastic.)
knowledge : • know the names of different materials used for building houses. • know that materials have similarities and differences. • know the meaning of the terms waterproof , transparent, opaque, rough, smooth, hard ,soft, bend, able to be stretched, bumpy, shiny and other terms that reflect observation of materials. • know the uses of common materials such as metal, glass, brick ,wood and plastic.	Feely Box Activities - Describe and guess the contents.(Paired activity .) Describe your material to someone who cant see it. Can they guess what it is ? Sorting Activities (Year 1 and Year 2) Look around locally for any building work. See how materials are being used. Trail -Maths and science looking at shape and materials used in construction
Skills: • To able to sort materials using observation skills. • To be able to record their observations in their own way. • To be able to describe what they have done and why . Describing similarities and differences between materials and in terms of shape , colour and texture. • To ask questions and look for the answers. • To work cooperatively in a group.	Building a class house (planning permission /technology) Sorting materials looking at similarities and differences -two sets Finding out about uses based on these characteristics 1.Set up waterproof experiment . Which materials are good for keeping the rain out ?
Attitudes : • To be trying to find out things for themselves • to enjoy learning and working with others. • to cooperate and collaborate with others.	2.Making windows -Which is the best material for windows ? 3.Is metal used inside and outside ? Why 4.How strong is wood ?

Medium-term plans: example of Year 3 half-termly plan

Medium-term plans: example of Year 1 half-termly RE plan

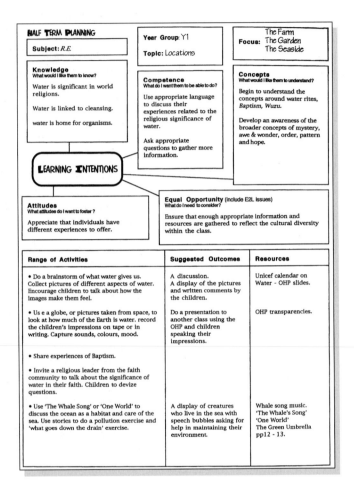

HALF TERM PLANNING		
Subject: *R.E.*	**Year Group:** Y1 **Topic:** Locations	**Focus:** The Farm The Garden The Seaside

Knowledge
What would I like them to know?

Water is significant in world religions.

Water is linked to cleansing.

water is home for organisms.

Competence
What do I want them to be able to do?

Use appropriate language to discuss their experiences related to the religious significance of water.

Ask appropriate questions to gather more information.

Concepts
What would I like them to understand?

Begin to understand the concepts around water rites, *Baptism, Wuzu*.

Develop an awareness of the broader concepts of mystery, awe & wonder, order, pattern and hope.

LEARNING INTENTIONS

Attitudes
What attitudes do I want to foster?

Appreciate that individuals have different experiences to offer.

Equal Opportunity (include E2L issues)
What do I need to consider?

Ensure that enough appropriate information and resources are gathered to reflect the cultural diversity within the class.

Range of Activities	Suggested Outcomes	Resources
• Do a brainstorm of what water gives us. Collect pictures of different aspects of water. Encourage children to talk about how the images make them feel.	A discussion. A display of the pictures and written comments by the children.	Unicef calendar on Water - OHP slides.
• Use a globe, or pictures taken from space, to look at how much of the Earth is water. record the children's impressions on tape or in writing. Capture sounds, colours, mood.	Do a presentation to another class using the OHP and children speaking their impressions.	OHP transparencies.
• Share experiences of Baptism.		
• Invite a religious leader from the faith community to talk about the significance of water in their faith. Children to devize questions.		
• Use 'The Whale Song' or 'One World' to discuss the ocean as a habitat and care of the sea. Use stories to do a pollution exercise and 'what goes down the drain' exercise.	A display of creatures who live in the sea with speech bubbles asking for help in maintaining their environment.	Whale song music. 'The Whale's Song' 'One World' The Green Umbrella pp12 - 13.

Title / Key Q's	Learning Intentions	PoS Links	Activities	Special Resources	Evaluation
What are the main differences between the sea, rivers, streams a waterfalls?	Knowledge: ① To know What is a river a where/ what is its source? ② Understanding Compare the differences between rivers, sea, streams, waterfalls & the different life forms which exists in each of the above. ③ Competence. To name, a locate major rivers etc. on a map. Attitude: Importance of rivers etc, a need to keep clean - Pollution.	Key Stage ② 1b, 2a. 3a. 3b. 3c. Study Unit 7 a & b. 10. a a b.	①. Look at pictures, etc. to locate local rivers a streams a then to move unto major rivers etc. on os. a mo ②. Characteristics - differences. ③. Travel. ④. Crossing rivers etc. ⑤ Life forms. ⑥ Pollution.	Videos, Photographs. O.S. Map. (local).	
Who were some of the famous explorers, inventors, a rulers from the Victorian times to the present day?	Knowledge:- ① To name a know their important discoveries ② The rel of their discoveries a how it effects	Key stage ② Victorians ③a 3a, b, c. Study Unit 3b 7a	①. To select 2 rulers, inventors a explorers. ②. Major contribution of each.	Videos. Photographs/ posters	

Medium-term plans: example of Year 3–4 termly geography and history plan

'*Learning Intentions' column first*, considering how far the children have, in general, fulfilled the learning intentions, then to decide whether the activities listed are still relevant. For instance, it is highly likely, with this approach, that some activities will no longer seem necessary because the children already understand or know the content. Alternatively, some of the activities might now seem too difficult, with a context too complex for the children to grasp. Looking at the activities in this critical way as the term is passing means that '*Assessment information is used to inform future planning*' – an essential OFSTED requirement. If we do not continually reconsider planned activities in the light of the learning intentions, we are taking no account of our assessment judgements and merely tripping through activities. In order to validate decisions to either remove or replace activities as the term progresses, there clearly needs to be some school policy decision made about how this would be shown on teachers' plans. A crossed-out activity could be initialled, for instance, with a brief reason given: '*clearly understood, no longer necessary*'. This is an important practice to establish, because, after plans have been monitored, scrutinised and signed by senior managers, the message seems to be that plans *must not then change*. If we are to truly '*use assessment information to inform future planning*' it is implicit that plans must be able to be modified.

The short-term plan

The purpose of the short-term plan is to be, first and foremost, a working tool for the class teacher, setting out the detail of the week to come so that lessons run smoothly, are well prepared and learning intentions are clear.

As in the medium-term plan, the plan must be essentially dynamic, including changes on a day-to-day basis, wherever the learning needs dictate that a lesson needs to be shorter, longer or changed altogether.

Most short-term plans are created on a weekly basis, with the content of each day filled in within this format. Some teachers plan every day in great detail before the week begins, whereas others plan the week roughly at first, filling in the detail as the week progresses. Both approaches are acceptable if the teaching and learning needs are fulfilled.

The format of the short-term plan is a continual headache in many schools, because rigid formats constrain the teacher from making the short-term plan a useful record. It is not uncommon for teachers to complete the school short-term plan in order to hand it in, then privately write their own, more important notes for their own use. If this is happening, the system is not working and time needs to be spent in designing a short-term plan which will provide a consistent school record but is also useful and flexible for teachers.

Ingredients of the short-term plan

The first step in resolving some of these difficulties is to decide on common ingredients for the short-term plan. These might consist of the following:

- the activities for the week, set out for each day
- organisation for the activities showing how children will work, whether in groups, pairs or individually and what children will actually be doing
- a breakdown of learning intentions, usually linked to each group's work (*differentiation by task*), or a string of learning intentions if the whole class is working at their own level, going through various stages (*differentiation by outcome*)
- what children with special needs will be doing
- use of other adults in the room
- the expected product outcome/s (whether the final outcome will be writing in an exercise book, an oral presentation, a summary comment, a poster, etc, etc.)
- time allocation for the activities, often shown as a timetable
- assessment notes (jottings about children who need more help/different work or for whom the activity was not challenging enough), sometimes recorded separately from the plan – *see further detail below.*

The way in which the teacher writes the plan varies according to the needs of the teacher: for some teachers bullet points are sufficient, whereas others prefer to write in prose form.

Assessment notes on the short-term plan

Assessment by omission is a powerful tool for gathering assessment information against the day-to-day learning intentions. The general situation for most of the class is that they achieve what you set out for them to achieve. In other words, they fulfil the learning intention of the task. There is, then, no need to write down for the bulk of the class this same information over and over again. What is important is to make brief notes about children for whom the work was inappropriate, who either did not fulfil the learning intention or fulfilled it to such an extent that they need further challenges. These notes feed directly into the next day's or week's planning and are the types of notes which teachers have been making for years. It needs to be recognised that these notes are formal assessment judgements, and form a continuous assessment record against the planned learning intentions for every subject of the National Curriculum. To then transfer this information onto individual children's records would take an enormous amount of time, so notes made on short-term plans seem to be the most manageable record of children's attainment which corresponds to the detail of the National Curriculum. This strategy appears to follow the statutory requirements for 'recording and retaining evidence' found in the QCA *Assessment and Reporting Arrangements* booklets:

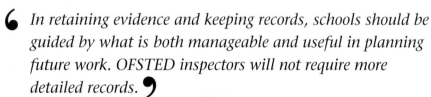

In retaining evidence and keeping records, schools should be guided by what is both manageable and useful in planning future work. OFSTED inspectors will not require more detailed records.

(QCA 1998)

Formats

Taking into account basic differences between staff such as size of handwriting and experience of teaching, the format needs to be flexible in the space used. There are several approaches.

The first approach is that, as long as the agreed ingredients are shown, teachers write their short-term plans in their preferred place: folders, booklets and so on. The plans can be photocopied for monitoring purposes, but will take longer to read, because of the variety. However, if we believe that monitoring needs should take second place to teaching and learning needs, this is inevitable.

The second approach is to have a common format, but one which is as open as possible, with as many follow-on sheets or different sized versions as people need.

The third approach is to have a set, structured format on one or two sides of paper. This can be a less effective approach, as teachers can find that they run out of space or feel that they should write more in the allocated space.

Because of the personal nature of the short-term plan, all the approaches above will work for some people and not for others.

By September 1999 it is likely that most teachers will have three different weekly/daily planning sheets:

- the Literacy Hour plan (session 1)
- the Numeracy Hour plan (session 2)
- the remaining time plan (session 3)

Monitoring

Monitoring demands have caused many of the problems associated with short-term plans, so it is necessary to explore some of the issues here.

The least effective monitoring strategy appears to be to receive plans from teachers, sign them and hand them back. The evidence suggests that most heads do not have time to read them thoroughly, have no way of knowing whether it then actually happens, and it encourages teachers to spend time writing for accountability reasons rather than for learning needs. When short-term planning is a new departure in a school it seems, however, the best strategy for getting teachers into the habit. However, once short-term planning is established, many schools relax the monitoring demands, preferring to see the plan on a termly basis during a face-to-face review/forecasting discussion or asking to see it when needed, such as when curriculum co-ordinators

Sheet 1

Activity Lesson including differentiation	Knowledge/Concepts	Skills	Equipment	A.T/I	Equal Opps. Grouping	Evaluation
Repeated Patterns. Discuss pattern on carpet get the children to predict what might come next using examples. The children to work having 3 goes at printing a pattern by themselves.	Pattern repeated. That it occurs again and again not once. Importance of using apron.	Writing name on work. Not mixing up colours when printing. Making a simple pattern.	Indian carved animals.	I	In pairs but individual work. Mixed sex.	Mubinya, Ashley, Venue of repeating didn't use a pattern. Anjana, Mehak, Emily able to print pattern using 3 animals.
Beads. Using bead cards. Making a pattern which repeats using a bead card either: With a repeated pattern A pattern to be repeated depending on ability	A repeated pattern.	Fine motor skills of threading.	bead tray + cards	I	In pairs. Individual work. New partner.	

Sheet 2

Activity Lesson including differentiation	Knowledge/Concepts	Skills	Equipment	A.T/I	Equal Opps. Grouping	Evaluation
Ladybird Game. Playing the game in h.s. Version 1 Using numbers + matching to 10 Version 2 Using spots + adding to 10 Version 3 Matching dots + digits ...cont...	Recognising digits. addition. Numberbonds to 10. to numbers to 10 adding. value of digit/number	Counting to 10. counting on. counting 1:1 counting. 1:1 matching. Working cooperatively in a group. in independently. rules.	Ladybird game. Cake game number dice dotted dice.	A.T.	Ability & grouping to fully assess ability of different children. Mixed ability groups	Activity was too complicated too many factors involved. Boring, good in chunks but small groups need more practical experience. Georgina + Emily + Tiye argued (develop social skills) understanding + independent working with Ruth, Ashley, Patricia, could not independently categories given had to ... into compartments.

Sheet 3

Activity Lesson including differentiation	Knowledge/Concepts	Skills	Equipment	A.T/I	Equal Opps. Grouping	Evaluation
Animated Alphabet	Matching objects with initial letter sounds.	Using direction arrows on the computer. Taking turns. knowledge of letter sounds	Computer	I	Equal ability to allow children to either use knowledge or to explore at own pace.	
Planting Seeds. To discuss as a whole class what a seed needs to grow. Discuss the concept of an experiment to explore what a seed needs to grow. To build on work from nursery on seeds. For children if they can to plan an experiment to prove that a plant needs light or water or soil to grow. Draw + what they did.	Seed needs light, soil, water to grow. experiment.	Organising Discuss. To wait turn to speak. Organising their own equipment. Planting a seed. Drawing to record what they have done.	Seeds Compost pots.	T. A.	Ability groups (from discussion) to allow independence to develop an experiment if able to.	Mehak, Chidi, Emily, Georgina, Billy, Ben, Tiye. Able to say what plants needed. Using a control for experiment to prove if need water. Able to organise own experiment. Ruth, Rushal, Patricia, Ashley. Needed help in getting equipment ready + planting seed. All able to draw experiment with adult help. Wrote a sentence (letter strings) to describe activity. (Imran v. interested improved work.)
PSH.E+ R.E. Owl Babies Read story to class. To discuss how it feels to be without mummy.	Being scared. Feeling lonely.	Listening to a story. Listening to each other taking turns to talk. Repeating what each other says.	Owl baby story	T	Whole class.	Emily, Chidi, Mehak able to give reasons for extend what they thought. Patricia, Rushal, Ashley, Mubinya not confident to speak in groups yet.

Short-term planning sheets

③ Maths Workshop Planning : Year 2

Groups	Date: Tues 10th March.	Assessment / Evaluation	Date: 11/3/98.	Assessment / Evaluation
Intro:	Demo of space/shape game: focus on adding strategies. →explicit.		Intro to ⊥ = square, right angle corners ⊥ < less more. N↘EW of cake/clock/90 °	
BINGO	(Wendy) PIP • use and understand the vocab of position and movement relating to PIP. – Record command panel and explanations.	All ok + Simon/Jim accurate. ↳ Jul/a apprehensive. Bashir some l.l. with Saria (Tries)	(Saria) • identify, name + define common 2D shapes. • use this knowledge to perform simple + → Play: 3 shape shape game.	Shapes fine. Still prob's — Faye with + Bashir Sausil Ferdous Saurul Rayna
HOPSCOTCH	(Hilary) PIP L.I. ditto – Record maps/directions of journey. – Record PIP instructions :Farhan.	Good 2D rep. lovely maps produced. → another way through?	• Sort 3D shapes according to props. • Make stable structures using 3D shapes. In pairs → Use 3D shapes to construct a model. Draw/Label shapes.	No.3 D prism pyramid Shaun Saurul all { cube cuboid Cylinder cone
SNAKES + LADDERS	(Shilpi) • identify, name and define common 2D shapes. • use this knowledge to perform related calculations. Play: 3 shapes shape game.	– shape props. all – sound ? adding strategies Niazul + Kamrau.	• Recognize a ⊥ in familiar context. Sort and record upper case wooden letters with a ⊥.	Samuel abs. Rahim Worked well ✓ Danny JS good
MONOPOLY.	• Identify 2D shapes as composite parts of 3D shapes. • identify + name 3D shapes (solid) 2D shapes (flat) → Match name to shape : use display to support. • Sort →2D →3D stick.	All OK (green) cone cylinder cuboid cube	x Rifat Dipak • Identify angles in shapes around the room as ⊥/larger/smaller x x	Rifat abs. Noohn Tomorrow more to Good abs and accurate ↗ larger measuring. > smaller All graped

Short-term plans: format for mathematics planning in Year 2

Bonne out. Elaine out.

Week Beginning: ① 23-2-98		Monday 23rd am pm	Tuesday 24th am pm	Wednesday 25th am pm	Thursday 26th am pm	Friday 27th am pm
Language and Literacy.	1.Big Book & Book Corner themes:	Lions:	(Helen to introduce both + the book 'Bringing the rain to Kapiti plains' Handa's surprise — introducing Story.			
		Tigers:	Extending story by questions relating to animal + fruit names; drawing attention to pattern on fabric.			
	TIGER'S ROOM 2.Letter of the week: Jj -introduce letter J with whole class using pictoral alphabet.	Simple letter shape formation sheet. - independent exploration of letter J shape reinforce class times + folio on alphabet + those whose names begin with		Letter J collage - cut out of sugar paper with coloured sticker/cotton wool		
	3.Alphabet Corner:	← Paper + pens + wooden letters. - independent exploration of letter shapes + own writing				
	4.Writing/ Drawing Activities: - general exploration of writing media - encourage children to draw themselves/family;	Large sugar paper -markers, pencils, wax crayons etc to add their own writing/write their own names		zigzag books- pencils/ felt pens.		blue sugar paper + chalks.
	5 & 6.Writing Opportunities: - independent use of Stamps + mini books encourage children to attempt own writing	Stamps (wild animals) -stamping animals onto book, Office area- paper trays, (role play writing -taking messages		stapled. small pieces of paper + pens, adding own writing pencils, pens etc -telephones from the phone etc.)		
	7.Computer (language based): - choice of activities within program ranging from alphabet song to matching letters with objects	Alphabet Workshop. -older/able children selecting activities from the desk top to include letter matching games.				
	8. Role-play/ Homecorner theme: -introducing African theme; looking at African fabrics -encourage children to draw on own experiences/family knowledge.	African Clothing theme — simple shop African theme Kitchen area- wooden pots/wicker baskets - decorate wall/sofa area with hessian fabric + photographs of Eritrea - places to sit on				
Science	9.Sand Themes: -to encourage exploration of wet sand + what it feels like; what you can do with it	← Buckets, scoops, moulds → wettish sand for moulding * showing children how to fill, flatten, bang out a sand castle/mould from bucket.				
	10.Water themes: -to explore pouring from + into different sized bottles; effective use of funnels	Selection of small, medium bottles + funnels * small wooden trolley by water tray for children to select equipment				
	11.Hands-on display theme: - to investigate how pieces fit together-best way to connect them	Wooden meccano new. * strips with holes in placed out with screws/nuts + other connector pieces separated out.		Wooden meccano -old set		

Bonne or Josie

Elaine

Short-term plans: format for nursery planning

Malik	Maths	**LION'S ROOM** 14. Number Hands-on display: - opportunity to look at numbers, match numbers, make lines of numbers	magnetic numbers /shapes + magnetic boards with small tray of paper + pens				
		15. Number/ Counting/ Sorting Activities: - selection of basic colour sorting; size sorting + ordering activities	small dinosaurs + coloured hexagons to match to	black boards + wooden cubes. - counting - organising	coloured cotton reels + thread - making patterns with large + small	links - piles of diff colours children to make chains of one colour	small fruit teddies buttons + sorting tubs
		16. Shape/ Colour Hands-on display: - focus on blue objects, construction etc for investigation	Blue table - different shades of blue colour with blue paper objects; blue construction; blue pens + white				
		17. Shape/ Colour/ Sorting Activities: Rectangle	Marian's: rectangle activities Drawing around rectangles	sticking rectangles on Jumper/Tshirt			▽
		18. Maths Puzzles/ Games; - confidence with matching + sorting shapes within inset or rod type shape sorter	Selection of wooden shape puzzles Shape sorters etc				
		19. Computer (maths based): - mouse skills, clicking + dragging + dropping items	Find Teddy ──────▷	Dress Teddy			
Josie (or lang.)	Imaginative play	20. Small world theme: (Table top/ Floor) - children to build, design a scene + tell story / narrate their own ideas as they play - independent + collaborative play	Duplo Zoo + Duplo farm - leaving mats free, with animals lined up etc ready for children to build scene as they wish. Duplo vehicles + bricks etc - pile of bricks - vehicles lined up, ready to be joined together or built upon				
	Aesthetic & creative	21. Modelling 3D (junk/ clay/ playdough etc):					
		22. Collage: (Helen) - small scale sticking/ painting extending fine motor skills - using African fabric - talking about pattern + colours		Making puppets from using African fabric	Handa's surprise		
		23. Graphics: - exploration of	rainbow crayons / chunky crayons Paper - range of colours + sizes				

Short-term plans: continuation of format for nursery planning

Book Focus Plan

Date: W/B Monday 9th March   Week 3

HELEN: cover.

CHARLIE TO MONITOR IT

1. Shared Text: Dan the Flying Man	Intro to genre: fiction Read.	Re-read up under on through in
		Alternative titles — know else could list more spellings of verbs — (ing) things
2.	Focus on plot sequence.	Can't use over must use another preposition. eg runing/jumping/hopping/bouncing

Recap plot sequence Where did DAN go.

Group	MONDAY	TUESDAY 10 March.	WEDNESDAY 11th March	THURSDAY 12th	FRIDAY 13th
Activities	Plan / Assessment	Plan / Assessment	Plan / Assessment	Plan / Assessment	Plan / Assessment

Yellow
A. Bashir
Shahida (lucky)
Farzana
Shaheda
Julfa
Rukshana
Ferdous
Samsul

- shared reading of BIG BOOK + Shilpi.

(Saria) Dan the Flying Man 6 + PIP
- Re-read text: identify rhymes
- Draw each place visited in plot + Dan.
- Complete journey questionnaire.
All can sequence gapfills. No time.

(Wendy)
- Use lg floor map to recap sequence of Journey
- Feed in instructions to PIP using prompt sheets/record and refine as we go on easel.
(Basher going to work some !:1.
Samsul ++ what will happen

(Saria)
- Work on individual journey questionnaires → share.
- make sentences → re-read
- Go over PIPs journey so far – add worksheets.

Blue
Faize
Noosheen
Nasir
Shaibul
Humayun
Rimi.
Farhan.

(Hilary) The Sandwich that Max Made.
Guided info. discussion about own preferences. Complete (6+7+8) list 8) s.w. content to

Noosheen map + adventure plotting route.
Farhan indepandance air computer COROM FIRST WORD.

(Hilary)
Ss read around gp. Look at unfamiliar words, jumbled sentence on card into 8+7+8
Dictionary wk.

(Hilary) Cloze activity all together & individually Write out our ingredients & method for sandwich making.

We're going to make some sandwiches and share them by following our recipe.

Red
Danny Basheh.
Rahim
Roisin
Rujna
Kamral
Shadik
Niazul

NB No partners org Ben

(Wendy) Quiet reading (sustained habit).
Lt sampling = Iqbal.

(Shilpi) Mother Bear Comes Home (19)
- Re-read chapter (2) in turns.
- Questions to complete.
CD ROM or dictionary definition
→ short story.
Roisin / some (Kamral.)
Begun - all know Mermaid CDROM tomorrow

(Moni) chapter (2) questions T/F
→ CD ROM dictionary (objects)
→ short story
Read 3rd story x
Roisin v slow
Kamral Feedback Good start

(Moni)
- Read story 3
- Mermaid stories T/F
- Read to each other.
Did this at end of session. speaking on their own. Some progress but slow. Not sure if this was done. Rujna – used scrab of text.

Green
Dilwar (bipot)
Zabed
Iqbal
Naeem Bdesh.
Saddik Sedgwick Partner
Rifat Absent
Rabby (S)
Saumah (6)

(Wendy) SPIDER PIE - Anne Cameron NOVEL.
- Intro to text about......
- Group read chap 1 (6s)
- Discuss - meaning
Dipot absent Good discussion

(Rahela) @ 11.00
- Re-read chap 1 aloud (for Dilw)
- In pairs Design a spider poster to include 5 pieces of info a diagram
Rifat absent
Labbi/Saddik v into text only shared

(Helen)
- Read chapter 2 aloud. (obs T/F)
- Discuss - especially noting new vocab.
- In pairs design spider posters: use info to texts.
Only Labbi making progress - regular absence from Rabby J - Lt disjointe
→ Left alone to do this don't know how this design topic

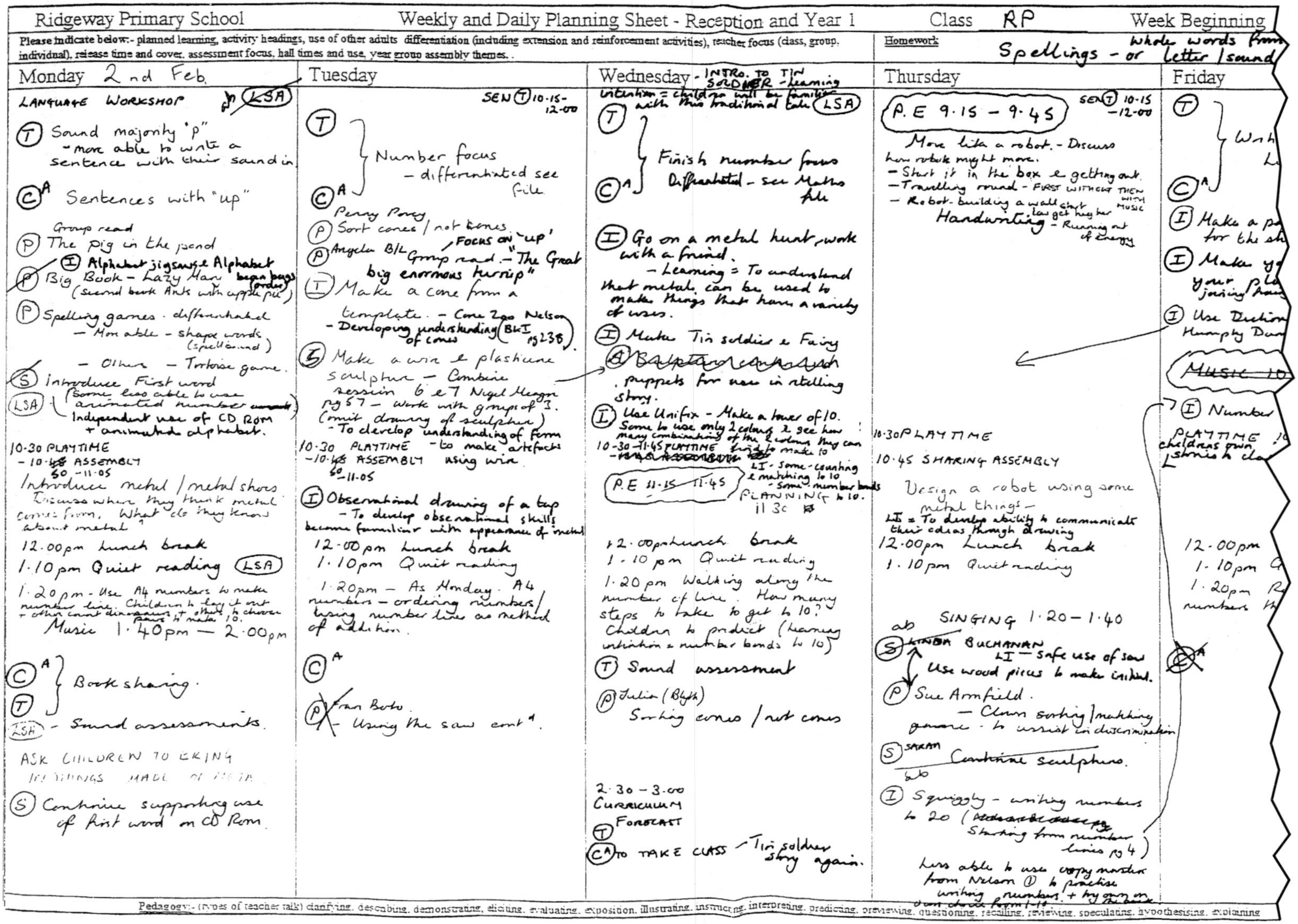
Ridgeway Primary School — Weekly and Daily Planning Sheet - Reception and Year 1 — Class RP — Week Beginning

Please indicate below:- planned learning, activity headings, use of other adults differentiation (including extension and reinforcement activities), teacher focus (class, group, individual), release time and cover, assessment focus, hall times and use, year group assembly themes.

Homework: Spellings - whole words from - or letter / sound

Monday 2nd Feb.

LANGUAGE WORKSHOP — LSA

(T) Sound majority "p" - more able to write a sentence with their sound in

(C)A Sentences with "up"

Group read
(P) The pig in the pond
(I) Alphabet jigsaw & Alphabet
(P) Big Book - Lazy Man (second book Ants with apple pie)
(P) Spelling games - differentiated - More able - shape words (spell sound) - Other - Tortoise game.
(S) Introduce First word (Some less able to use animated number)
(LSA) Independent use of CD Rom + animated alphabet.

10-30 PLAYTIME - 10.50 ASSEMBLY - 11-05
Introduce metal / metal shoes. Discuss where they think metal comes from. What do they know about metal?
12.00pm lunch break
1.10pm Quiet reading (LSA)
1.20pm - Use A4 numbers to make number line. Children to lay it out + other count dinosaurs + others to choose pairs to make 10.
Music 1.40pm — 2.00pm

(C)A (T) Book sharing.
(LSA) - Sound assessments.
ASK CHILDREN TO BRING IN THINGS MADE OF METAL
(S) Continue supporting use of first word on CD Rom.

Tuesday

SEN (T) 10.15 - 12.00

(T) (C)A Number focus - differentiated see file.

Percy Porcy
(P) Sort cones / not cones
(P) Angela B/L Group read. - "The Great big enormous turnip" — FOCUS ON "up"
(I) Make a cone from a template. - Cone Zoo Nelson - Developing understanding of cones (BLT pg 238)
(I) Make a wire & plasticine sculpture - Combine session 6 & 7 Nigel Meager pg 57 - work with groups of 3. (omit drawing of sculpture) - To develop understanding of form - to make artefacts using wire

10.30 PLAYTIME - 10.50 ASSEMBLY - 11.05
(I) Observational drawing of a toy - To develop observational skills become familiar with appearance of metal
12.00pm Lunch break
1.10pm Quiet reading
1.20pm - As Monday. A4 numbers - ordering numbers / using number line as method of addition.

(C)A
(P) Fran Boto - Using the saw cont'd.

Wednesday - INTRO. TO TIN SOLDIER - Learning intention = children will be familiar with this traditional tale (LSA)

(T) (C)A Finish number focus. Differentiated - see Maths file

(I) Go on a metal hunt, work with a friend. - Learning = To understand that metal can be used to make things that have a variety of uses.
(I) Make Tin soldier & Fairy puppets for use in retelling story.
(I) Use Unifix - Make a tower of 10. Some to use only 2 colours & see how many combinations of the 2 colours they can find to make 10 - LI - Some counting & matching to 10 - Some number bonds to 10.
10-30 - 11.45 PLAYTIME
P.E 11.15 - 11.45
PLANNING 11.30
12.00pm Lunch break
1.10pm Quiet reading
1.20pm Walking along the number of line. How many steps to take to get to 10? Children to predict (learning intuition & number bonds to 10)
(T) Sound assessment
(P) Julia (Blyth) Sorting cones / not cones
2.30 - 3.00 CURRICULUM FORECAST
(T) (C)A TO TAKE CLASS - Tin soldier story again.

Thursday

P.E 9.15 - 9.45 — SEN (T) 10.15 - 12.00
Move like a robot. - Discuss how robots might move.
- Start it in the box & getting out.
- Travelling round - FIRST WITHOUT THEN WITH MUSIC
- Robot building a wall start low get higher
Handwriting - Running out of Energy

10.30 PLAYTIME
10.45 SHARING ASSEMBLY
Design a robot using some metal things - LI = To develop ability to communicate their ideas through drawing
12.00pm Lunch break
1.10pm Quiet reading
SINGING 1.20 - 1.40
(S) BUCHANAN LI - Safe use of saw. Use wood pieces to make cricket.
(P) Sue Armfield. - Class sorting / matching game - to assist in discrimination
(S) SARAH Continue sculptures.
(I) Squiggly - writing numbers to 20 (Starting from number lines pg 4)
Less able to use copy master from Nelson (1) to practise writing numbers + try own on [illegible]

Friday

(T) (C)A Writ[...]
(I) Make a p[...] for the s[...]
(I) Make yo[...] your pl[...] joining ha[...]
(I) Use Dictio[...] Humpty Dum[...]
MUSIC 10
(I) Number[...]
PLAYTIME 1[...] childrens own stories to cla[...]
12.00pm
1.10pm
1.20pm
numbers

Pedagogy:- (types of teacher talk) clarifying, describing, demonstrating, eliciting, evaluating, exposition, illustrating, instructing, interpreting, predicting, previewing, questioning, recalling, reviewing, speculating, hypothesising, explaining

Short-term plans: format for Reception/Year 1 weekly plan

spend time in a classroom monitoring. Although all adults involved in the week's teaching should, ideally, be either involved in the planning or be very familiar with the short-term plan, it seems unwise to write short-term plans in order for a supply teacher to be able to take the class. The purpose of the plan is to be a complete document for the class teacher, including planning and assessment decisions, and it should indicate basic intentions of coverage for a supply teacher, rather than step-by-step lesson plans which would be extremely difficult for a teacher new to the class to be able to follow.

Short-term planning in the Early Years (Nursery and Reception)

In *Looking at Children's Learning*, a booklet giving guidance for planning and learning against the *Desirable Outcomes*, the following ingredients of the short-term plan are recommended for consideration, although not all would need to be recorded on the plan, but may well be recorded elsewhere:

- *how each activity builds on the children's previous experiences, interests and achievements*

- *the purpose of each activity*

- *which aspect(s) within the area(s) of learning provide the focus for the activity*

- *which Desirable Outcomes provide the specific focus for the intended learning*

- *the nature of the evidence of children's learning that would be expected to result from each activity*

- *the teacher's role and that of other staff in both the activity itself and in gathering evidence of children's learning*

- *how they will communicate to the children the purpose of each activity and their expectations*

■ *the resources and equipment that will be needed*

■ *the number of children that could take part in each activity and how they will manage this group of children in the context of a larger group or class*

■ *the balance of teacher directed and child initiated activities.* **9**

(SCAA 1997)

It is also suggested that teachers *'should be aware of opportunities that arise for children to demonstrate their knowledge, skills and understanding that have not been anticipated or planned.'* The booklet goes on to say that this may lead to *'adjusting the day-to-day plans'* which emphasises that, at all stages, the plan must be a dynamic instrument.

2 Sharing Learning Intentions with Children

Over the last few years, especially since OFSTED requires it on their inspections, it has become more commonplace for teachers to share learning intentions with children. It has not, however, been part of the traditional culture of our educational system to do this. Indeed some research carried out by Willes (1983), of children entering a reception class, reinforced the notion that children very quickly learn simply to respond to instructions by the teacher:

> *...finding out what the teacher wants, and doing it, constitute the primary duty of a pupil.*
>
> (Willes 1983)

We have always been very good at telling children what we want them to do and how we want them to do it, thus establishing control and discipline, an essential element when teaching a number of children at once. Without the 'secret' knowledge of the learning intention, however, children have been deprived of information which will not only enable them to carry out the task more effectively, they have also been denied the opportunity to self-evaluate, communicate this to the teacher, set targets for themselves and get to understand their own learning needs: in other words, to think intelligently about their own learning, rather than 'finding out what the teacher wants, and doing it'.

Knowing the learning intention for every task is, it seems, a child's basic right as a learner. Crooks (1988), as a result of his review of studies involving formative assessment in action, stated that *'the most vital of all the messages'* emerging from the review was that assessments must emphasise the skills knowledge and attitudes (learning intentions) which the teacher believed were most important.

Giving children only the 'what' and 'how', *without* the learning intention, might look something like this:

The rainbow activity

*'Today I want you to paint a picture of a rainbow. (***'what'***) Here is the chart of the rainbow colours that we have been looking at this week. You will be given a piece of white paper, a long, flat-headed brush and some water-colours. Make it the most beautiful rainbow you can. (***'how'***)*

I have given no focus or purpose, so there are now many unanswered questions in children's minds, such as:

'Will I get told off if I use only part of the paper, or must I fill it up?'
'Can I have other things in the picture, or will it matter if it is just a rainbow?'
'What does beautiful mean? Should it be very bright colours or could I make it faint and watery?'
etc.

Children often hear all the words spoken by the teacher but still feel unsure about what they have to do – they don't know what you are really looking for.

This situation manifests itself in several ways:

One or two children will come and ask what it is they have got to do, usually resulting in an exasperated teacher either telling them to ask another child or repeating the instructions as before. (Some children will always do this, whether you share learning intentions or not!)

A number of time-wasting tactics emerge, such as some children going to the toilet, some falling off their chairs and some sharpening their pencils.

Most children, however, do the simplest thing possible: they wait. They wait until the child nearest to them, who is generally a safe bet in getting things right, starts the task, then take a lead from that child. This is often why several children's work will look similar when seated together.

The same lesson, now including the shared learning intention:

'Today I want you to paint a picture of a rainbow. ('what') *Here is the chart of the rainbow colours that we have been looking at this week. You will be given a piece of white paper, a long, flat-headed brush and some water-colours. Make it the most beautiful rainbow you can. ('how')*

'The only thing I want you to focus on, and it is the reason for you painting the rainbow, is to practise using your brush to blend each of the colours of the rainbow together. You are practising the skill of using your brush to blend colours, an important skill in art.' ('why')

LI after inst.

Notice that the focus comes *after* the instructions. Teachers often include the learning intentions focus within the instructions of the task, which can be muddling. It seems clearer to state the focus (or what you are looking for) after the instructions (e.g. *'Now, I've told you what to do. This is what I'm looking for and why you are doing this . . . So what am I looking for? Why are we doing this?'*)

Repeat.

Sharing learning intentions means that children are much more likely to get straight on with the task, will be more focused and so on. However, the teacher does need to know the learning intention of the tasks in the first place.

Finding the right words

LI.
Ched sp

Explaining the learning intention takes very little time, and is said at the same time as children are told what to do and how to do it. However, the learning intention needs to be shared in a way which makes it clear to the child, so it is usually necessary to convert the intention into 'child speak'.

focus
adjectives

Teachers trying this out have found that the way a learning intention is shared is mainly by stating first what the **focus** of the work should be. For instance, children asked to write a story might be told that the main thing they should put their efforts into would be to choose the best adjectives they

Why

task - diff. focus.
basic LI

EYr product outcome.

LI for investigation

process skills

can. Although this has made the focus clear, the children still do not know why they are being asked to do this. The next thing to say, therefore, would be that the reason for this activity is for them to improve the adjectives they use to make their writing more interesting and give a clearer picture to the reader. This means that many tasks will have a different focus, but the same basic learning intention. It is important that children know both things: what they must concentrate on and the purpose of the task. Teachers of children in the Early Years often find that the way a learning intention is shared is by expressing the focus of the task in terms of the product outcome. For instance, with the learning intention of *'sequencing a story correctly'* the teacher might share this with children by saying *'The thing I am looking for is whether you can put the pictures of the little red hen into the right order to tell the story.'*

Sharing learning intentions for investigative tasks can be worrying, because it seems that you will have to tell children exactly what you wanted them to discover! The preferred way of making the purpose clear to the children is to state the learning intention in more general terms (*'The reason you are doing this is to find out more about what exercise does to the heart'*) or to focus on particular process skills (*'I want to see how well you can organise your investigation'*).

Sharing learning intentions is clearly easier with subjects the teacher is more confident about. The more rigorous and explicit the learning intentions in the medium-term plan, the easier it is. It may be, however, that subject co-ordinators could have a role in helping teachers clarify how they might share learning intentions. A very supportive strategy is to have a staff meeting where teachers bring along their short-term plans for the week. They are asked, in pairs, to each choose an activity which they have not yet done, to say what the learning intention of the activity is and then to work together on the exact form of words for sharing this with children. The resulting statements are read out. This exercise helps teachers to see common ways of sharing learning intentions, and it is a platform for various issues to be discussed.

The following examples of learning intentions being converted to 'child-speak', giving both the focus and the overall purpose, come from teachers across the age range:

ACTIVITY 3.

Learning Intention: To learn about repeated addition.

Words used:
'I want you to tell me an easier way of working out how many eyes you would need for five teddies. This will help you to add up the same number quickly.'

Learning Intention: To be aware of how Anne Fine develops characters.

Words used:
'What I want to know is <u>how</u> you know what the chicken is like. The reason you are doing this is because it will help you to find interesting ways to describe characters in your stories.'

Learning Intention: To find out the role played by the different parts of the digestive system.

Words used:
'What I am looking for is whether you can explain the journey of food from entry to exit using the names for each body bit. This will help you to understand how your body works.'

Learning Intention: To begin to use initial letter sounds as an aid to decoding unfamiliar words.

Words used:
'What I want to know is if you can't read a word can you say the beginning sound? This will help you guess or find the word.'

Learning Intention: To be able to use the past tense in writing.

Words used:
'I will be reading your work to see if you can use the past tense so that your writing makes sense. This will help you to be able to write more clearly.'

Learning Intention: To understand the sources of water evaporation.

Words used:
'The reason for this activity is because I want you to know all the different things that give off water and to see what happens to the water because you will then understand more about the importance of water in our world.'

Learning Intention: Pupils will know that the economic activities of settlements reflect their location and characteristics.

Words used:
'I want you to remember that what a settlement is like makes a difference to what jobs are available there. This will help you to understand how and why places are different from each other.'

Learning Intention: To be able to use their knowledge of insulation in setting up a fair test.

Words used:
'What I'm looking for is how you have recorded the investigation making every stage you went through very clear. This is to improve your investigation skills and to show me what you know about insulation.'

Learning Intention: To make a container to hold a specific object (a bag with a handle to hold a packet of crisps).

Words used:
'The most important thing for you to do is to be able to actually fit the crisps into the bag.'

> **Learning Intention:** To be able to use trial and improvement methods in solving a mathematical problem.
>
> **Words used:**
> *'The most important thing about this activity is trying out the different calculations to solve the problem and recording them. This will give you another way of working out the answer to a problem.'*

> **Learning Intention:** To understand the use of the Bible in guiding Christians.
>
> **Words used:**
> *'I want you to find the ten commandments and write down three examples of the way they are used in our school. The reason you are doing this is for you to see how the Bible guides Christians in their everyday life.'*

It seems important to make it clear to the children that, from now on, telling them the purpose or learning intention of every task will take place. Many teachers feel that they already share learning intentions for many lessons, but in an almost incidental way. It is when the learning intention is made explicit to children that it appears to have the greatest impact on their learning. If sharing learning intentions is a new departure for a teacher, it can be easy to forget to do it, and it takes about two weeks for it to become automatic. Strategies for making the learning intentions explicit and remembering to do it include:

- writing the activities for the day/week on the white board/flip chart, etc, with the learning intentions alongside them, so they are a constant reminder to children

- with younger children, reminding them throughout the lesson of the purpose

- asking children to remind you if you forget to tell them the learning intention (this works very well!)

- making it a whole school commitment, establishing in assembly that this will now happen in the classroom

explicit LI

■ making it school policy, once children can write reasonably fluently, that the learning intention is always written under the title of any piece of work. (This has further advantages for marking, dealt with in the next chapter.)

Feedback from teachers shows that a maximum of two learning intentions should be shared for every task, or the effect is diluted and children do not focus on any of them clearly. This means, therefore, that to give a main learning intention and then add *'and don't forget your spelling, capital letters, full stops and punctuation'* means we are in fact giving a whole string of learning intentions. This, of course, opens up a complex debate about children's writing and what we should expect, but one thing is clear: very few adults can focus on all aspects of their writing at once. Drafting provides the answer to many pieces of writing, where, in effect, a different learning intention is given for each stage of the drafting, but what about other areas of the curriculum, when writing is required? If we give children a clear science learning intention, for instance, but say we want good handwriting and so on, it is quite likely that children will put most of their efforts into the aspect which seems to matter most to the teacher. If the teacher continually criticises children's presentation, this will be communicated to them as the main learning intention of the task. There needs to be clear school policy about sharing learning intentions and it should be clear to all teachers and parents that because the focus of a piece of writing is not, say, spelling, on one day, it is likely to be the focus on a subsequent day.

The impact of sharing learning intentions

From the teacher's point of view, having to share learning intentions is a good discipline for having to be sure about the purpose of every task children are asked to do, and, to begin with, sometimes requires teachers to go back over their plans and make learning intentions more explicit. Of course, if they have been worked on by the staff and co-ordinators as described in the previous chapter, much of the work has been done before.

Teachers who have made explicit to children that this will happen and ensure that it is an automatic part of setting children off on an activity, often report dramatic changes in the culture of the classroom and in children's application and attitude to their work and learning.

The impact of sharing learning intentions, according to many teachers who have this firmly established as part of their teaching, is as follows:

- Children are more focused on the task.

- Children will persevere for longer.

- The quality of children's work improves.

- Behaviour, especially time-wasting tactics at the beginnings of lessons, improves.

- The dialogue between children while they are working is more likely to focus on the learning intention than on their own interests.

- Children become automatically self-evaluative, subconsciously or consciously weighing up how well they are doing against the learning intention.

- Marking is easier.

Where learning intentions have been shared for about a term, teachers report that children 'demand'/need the learning intention as a necessary part of the instructions for a task. I interviewed some children, asking them why they were being given the learning intention. Their responses were similar: they looked at me with disbelief and said, *'How can you do your work if you don't know why you're doing it?'*

Some children also begin to negotiate the appropriateness of the activity to fulfil the learning intention! This usually takes the form of changing resources or ways of working (e.g. *'If that's what I'm learning, wouldn't it be better if I got a number line instead?'/'I think I'd do that better if I worked on my own/with someone else.'*) In these schools, the children have developed beyond the 'sponge' model of being a pupil to actively considering their place and their needs for learning. I believe this should be one of our primary aims in teaching.

Finally, it is useful to trace the learning intention through its various stages, from the Programmes of Study to marking.

The following chart tracks 'the journey of a learning intention':

THE JOURNEY OF THE LEARNING INTENTION	PURPOSE	CHARACTERISTICS
Programmes of Study or *Desirable Outcomes*	Sets out the original aim for learning	General statement
Schemes of work	Is one of a progression of skills and concepts to be tackled for every year	The statement is broken down to make it clearer and more focused
Medium-term plan	Is taken from the scheme of work to create a teaching overview for the term in order to ensure that the teacher chooses or creates focused activities	Is as explicit as possible: starts with *'to know'*, *'to be able to'*, etc, and clarifies definitions of fuzzy words
Short-term plan	Ensures that the teacher knows the purpose of every task and the aim for different groups so that activities are well focused. Also enables assessment notes to be recorded against the learning intentions for the class or groups, for those who need more help or more challenge.	The original learning intention either stays the same as in the medium-term plan or is broken into perhaps four learning intentions (e.g. *'To understand place value to 100'* might break down into four aspects of place value to correspond with four ability groups)
Shared with children	To inform children of the purpose and focus of the task	Is converted into 'child-speak', so that it makes sense to the child. Is told after the instructions of the task and made explicit by writing on the board, etc.
Used for marking	Gives focused feedback to children and enables marking to form an assessment record	Teacher's comments or codes reflect the learning intention of the task and/or the child writes the learning intention under or as the title

Developing success criteria

For some subjects it can be helpful to encourage children to brainstorm the success criteria for a task. Dorothy Grange (Northumberland LEA) has influenced many teachers over the last few years in this initiative.

Her process is as follows:

1   *Establish the learning intention of the task*

2   *Ask the children* **'How will I know that you have achieved that?'***, inviting ideas, guided by the teacher. It is important that the children are involved in developing the success criteria, but the teacher can play 'Devil's Advocate' in order to refine them. In cases where the children need a degree of prior knowledge to be able to construct the success criteria, the teacher writes her own criteria first, then invites the children to contribute their ideas, then matches their ideas with hers. The teacher clearly needs to have the final word, after consultation with the children.*

3   *In the lesson review, individually, whole class, group or through partnership marking (see chapter 3) ask children how far they met the success criteria.*

Examples of success criteria (both from Middle schools)

Example 1: Activity + pupil response sheet

Learning Objectives:

■ *To know the difference between direct and indirect speech*

■ *To understand why an author would use both*

■ *To be able to write direct speech in a way that would interest the reader*

Activity
Read a passage from class novel which contains direct and indirect speech.

Discuss the differences and why the author would change from one to the other.

Children in groups to act out what they think was said in the passage which is written as indirect speech (photocopy of passage given out so that they can annotate it).

Individuals to write out their ideas as direct speech which would fit into the context of the rest of the dialogue from the book.

Teacher to model first part with class and discuss how the success criteria can be used to extend the children's skill in writing dialogue. (Success criteria and learning objectives as shown on pupil response sheet.)

Pupils and teacher to use response sheet to assess work when finished.

PUPIL RESPONSE SHEET   Name.............................
Title: Direct Speech
Learning Objectives:
   To know the difference between direct and indirect speech
   To understand why an author would use both
   To be able to write direct speech in a way that would interest the reader

Success criteria
I will have tried: I am pleased with . . .

  • to punctuate speech correctly

  • to use adverbs

  • to put the speech in different places in the sentence

  • to add description to show how the characters react to what is being said and how they behave when they are speaking

My next target will be:

Teacher comment

Example 2: Differentiation through use of success criteria

Learning Objective: To know about religious change in Tudor times	
Majority of class	**More able group**
Must show that you have used books to find appropriate information (dates and names)	**Must** give a description of events and reasons leading to Henry's break with Rome
Should describe the events that led to Henry's break with Rome	**Should** say how you think different groups of people would feel about the changes
Could give three reasons why Henry closed the monasteries	**Could** predict what you think will happen next
Feedback session (Some form of response partner work)	

An example of a nursery activity, where success criteria were used

The children were asked to make Christmas cards, with the learning intention given for them to learn how to use glue and glitter properly. The teacher asked the children why they were making the cards, and they replied *'So we can learn how to use glue and glitter properly.'*

The teacher next asked *'So how will I know if you have used the glue and glitter properly?'* There followed a number of ideas, such as *'There will be no glue on our hands'* and *'The glue won't be in blobs.'*

The children made their cards and, at the end of the session, the teacher gathered them together, repeated the learning intention and success criteria then asked them to show her how well they had used the glue and glitter. She chose one child at a time, asking the rest of the class, *'How well has . . . done?'* The children then asked that child to show them her hands and so on.

The point Dorothy makes is that children need to know what success might look like. If they don't achieve success in all aspects, the plenary provides a supportive environment for modelling the ways in which they could have achieved success. The teacher, at this point, is also made aware of the needs and achievements of the children, possibly providing a way forward for the creation of criteria for individual targets.

Although success criteria go a long way to informing children of what success means, it is also our teaching which informs children of the definition of success. For instance, if the purpose of an activity was for children to write something funny, the teaching leading up to this would have presumably consisted of introducing the class to funny passages from books, funny poems and so on, with related discussion and analysis about what had made it funny. Without previous teaching, we could otherwise be expecting children to invent success criteria for something about which they have limited knowledge or understanding.

Training children to think self-evaluatively

Children becoming self-evaluative is the next issue to discuss, because, once we enable children to become self-evaluative, we need to equip them with the skills to be able to communicate their thoughts to us. This needs focused training, but will lead to teacher and child establishing a valuable partnership for learning. Many studies have found that self-evaluation improves achievement. Research by Schunk (1996), in which self-evaluation was combined with learning goals, showed that children's persistence, achievement and self-esteem was improved. Black and Wiliam's important research about formative assessment found, as one of its conditions, that

> *For formative assessment to be productive, pupils should be trained in self-assessment so that they can understand the main purposes of their learning and thereby grasp what they need to do to achieve.*

(Black and Wiliam 1998)

Without being taught how to think evaluatively, children search for the answer the teacher wants when asked questions such as *'What did you think about your work?'* Typically, children will answer evaluative questions with superficial answers such as *'It was OK/I liked it/I could improve my handwriting.'* This is not only limited in its value, but can be counter-productive, encouraging children with low self-esteem to criticise their efforts too harshly.

A practical start is to make a poster of a list of evaluative questions which will be displayed in the classroom as a constant reminder to teacher and child.

A good set of questions could include the following:

- ◼ *What did you find easy?*

- ◼ *What did you find difficult/where did you get stuck? What helped you get out of the difficulty? (Was it something a **friend** said or did, something the **teacher** did, something to do with **equipment**, something you did **yourself**?)*

- ◼ *What do you need more help with?*

- ◼ *What are you most pleased with?*

- ◼ *Have you learnt anything new?*

- ◼ *How would you change this activity for another group/class?*

- ◼ *Do you have any questions?*

A training period begins, consisting of whole class discussions at the end of lessons, where the teacher picks out some of these questions and **gives examples of the kinds of answers children might give**, before inviting children to give answers. To give models of concrete examples of possible answers is a way of helping children to understand what is meant by thinking analytically and evaluatively. The teacher might therefore say:

❝ *Did anyone find any part of the task difficult – did they get stuck at anything then find a way to get out of that difficulty? For instance, you might have found it difficult to hold the brush so that it was easy to blend the colours, then noticed that the person next to you was holding it a different way, or you might have discovered this for yourself, or maybe I told you. You had a difficulty, but you learnt something new because of it! Or maybe you found it difficult to get the colours mixed properly . . . Now – would anyone like to say where they had difficulties and what helped them move on?* **"**

Focusing on points of difficulty and what helped children move on is at the heart of the learning process, so would be important questions to ask on a regular basis. By encouraging children to reveal these points as celebrations of new learning liberates them from perceiving difficulties as failures rather than as necessary to learning.

With this sort of practice, the teacher can start to introduce different platforms for self-evaluation as well as whole class discussion. After the training period, children can be encouraged to, at the end of lessons, over just a few minutes, think first, then make a self-evaluative comment to the person sitting next to them, listening to each other's comment in turn. They could either be given one of the questions from the poster or be invited to choose one themselves. Alternatively, children can write their own self-evaluation at the end of their work, again choosing or being given a question, whatever the subject. As children's writing becomes more fluent, this would be an important routine to establish throughout the school. The child's evaluative comment then becomes the first 'marking' of the work and forms part of the child's ongoing assessment record. However, the recording of the self-evaluation is considerably less important than the process itself, so should not become another record keeping burden. In the Early Years, self-evaluation is essentially oral, although, where marking takes place with the child, the self-evaluative comment could be recorded by the teacher. The age of the child is irrelevant when establishing sharing learning intentions and encouraging self-evaluation, although young children's comments will naturally take a more simplified form in the early stages.

Introducing the sharing of learning intentions and having a period of self-evaluation at the end of lessons links very well with the government's literacy and numeracy hours, in which the format of a lesson is supposed to include an introduction and a plenary.

By the time children are at the upper end of the primary school, it can be extremely worthwhile to introduce 'self-assessment journals' to be written during the last half hour of the week. A 'stream of consciousness' is not particularly helpful, but a reflective comment against the learning intentions of the week and the week's lessons have proved invaluable to teachers in guiding their planning for the following week.

How do you know when they know it?

Teachers use a variety of skills, especially questioning, observation and classroom testing to establish the extent to which children have learnt and understood. More open questions are more likely to yield fuller answers from children than closed questions and various strategies such as including the words *'do you think'* in a question (e.g. *'How do you think this works?'* rather than *'How does this work?'*) and leaving a five-second 'wait time' can encourage all children to respond to questions.

Black and Wiliam (1998), in their extensive review of literature on formative assessment, found that one study had led to a set of indicators or 'potential clues' to the level of a child's understanding being generated by the teachers involved. *'How do I really know the child understands?'* is a constant question for the teacher. The list gives some interesting clues:

❝ 1 *changes in demeanour: students who had understood were 'bright eyed' while those who had not appeared half-hearted;*

2 *extension of a concept: students who have understood something often take the idea further on their own initiative;*

3   *making modifications to a pattern: students who understand spontaneously start making their own modifications, while those who don't understand imitate or follow rules;*

4   *using processes in a different context: students who have understood a particular idea often start seeing the same patterns elsewhere;*

5   *using shortcuts: only students who are sure of the 'big picture' can shortcut a procedure so that thinking up or using a short cut is taken as evidence of understanding;*

6   *ability to explain: students who have understood something are usually able to explain it;*

7   *ability to focus attention: persistence on a task is taken as a sign of understanding.* ❞

(Reynolds *et al* 1995, in Black and Wiliam 1998)

3 Marking and feedback

Marking has the potential to be the most powerful, manageable and useful ongoing diagnostic record of achievement. It is a manageable way of tracking National Curriculum learning intentions for written work for individual children on a day-to-day basis along with notes made on the short-term plan to feed into further planning. However, it is also a very effective medium for providing feedback to children about their progress. Thus, marking has essentially two functions: to provide an assessment record and to provide feedback to the child.

Marking as an assessment record

Since the Dearing Review of 1993, SCAA/QCA *Assessment and Reporting Arrangements* booklets for Key Stages 1 and 2 have included a reference to marking in the statutory requirements for Teacher Assessment:

> *Decisions about how to mark work and record progress are professional matters for schools to consider in the context of the needs of their children.*
>
> (SCAA/QCA/DFEE 1994 onwards)

This sentence provides the only reference to assessment strategies. The move to include marking as a strategy was deliberate: to encourage more manageable record keeping, which would also provide feedback to the child. A critical advantage of marking as a record is that it is owned by the child, thus is more likely to have an impact on learning. Records kept at a distance from the child tend to have little impact on learning.

Practical strategies

In order for learning intentions to be tracked, the words of the learning intentions need to appear somewhere on the work. Having the learning intention under the title of the piece gives it meaning. It is often the case that looking back through exercise books over previous work can be fairly meaningless without an indication of the purpose of the activity. Two possibilities for making the learning intention visible are as follows:

For children who can write reasonably fluently

1   **Ask the child to write the learning intention under the title and the date.** This could be school policy so that it is expected practice by teachers and children. Learning

The learning intention written on the work

intentions on work transform pages in exercise books, making them infinitely more meaningful both for the child at the time and for the teacher when looking back at work.

2 When the work is marked, *a very brief, general comment is made by the side of the learning intention* such as very well achieved, achieved, needs more help, perhaps initialled by the teacher. Codes could serve just as well for this purpose.

For children who are too young or unable to write fluently

There needs to be a marking comment at the end of the work which includes the words of the learning intention [e.g. *'You have set out a letter in the correct way'* (where the learning intention of the tasks was *to be able to use the conventional form of formatting a letter*)]

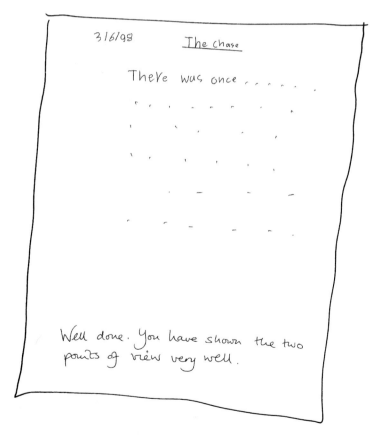

The learning intention included in the marking comment

These strategies reinforce the learning intention for the teacher and the child and focus the marking on how well the learning intention has been achieved.

Marking as feedback

Formative assessment means that the assessment information has some impact on both teaching and learning, and, at its best, involves the child. The previous chapter dealt with the child as an evaluator after being told the learning intention of the task. Marking, and how marked work is followed up with the child, can play a further part in involving the child in improving and moving forward. Sadler (1989) identified that, in order for improvement to take place, the child must first know the purpose of the task, then how far this was achieved, and finally be given help in knowing how to move closer towards the desired goal or 'in closing the gap'. It is perhaps in the last aspect that we have not always helped children to maximise their achievement. Tunstall and Gipps' research project *Teacher Feedback to Young Children* (1996), identified a number of ways in which teachers give feedback to children: rewarding and punishing, approving and disapproving, specifying attainment and specifying improvement, and constructing achievement and constructing the way forward. The last two categories are particularly interesting. Their definitions are as follows:

> **Specifying attainment** is teacher feedback which identifies specific aspects of successful attainment . . .
> **Specific improvement** identifies where mistakes lie and how work can be improved.
>
> (Tunstall and Gipps 1996)

In both these types the feedback is directed from the teacher to the child, with the teacher telling the child what is good or present in the work/activity and what can be done to improve.

> *Constructing achievement* is . . . *undertaken much more in conversation or discussion with the child. . . . With this type of feedback, teachers drew the child into explaining or demonstrating achievement using the child's work; it also drew on and developed children's own self-assessment.* **Constructing the way forward** *was used to articulate future possibilities in a learning partnership with the child. This type of feedback provided children with strategies that they could adopt to develop their work, and it encouraged children to assess their own work.*
>
> (Stobart and Gipps 1997)

Effective marking can be reflected in all of these types of feedback. Specifying attainment and improvement most commonly takes the form of written feedback or marking whereas constructing achievement and the way forward most often takes the form of some kind of dialogue, either with teacher and child alone or in the context of a group or the whole class. Much of the previous section on training children to become analytically self-evaluative links with constructing achievement and the way forward, especially if the child is made aware of or evolves future strategies for success.

Traditional marking

Typically teachers with younger children find it easier to mark children's work with them, thus discussing the issues in full. The main reason this is possible is probably because younger children write less, and the issues involved in the quality of their writing are fewer than for older children. The older the child, the more likely it is that the teacher is forced to mark away from the child, mainly because there is more content and more to say to the child. Teachers want to give children as much information as possible about their work, so the classic scenario is that the teacher spends a great deal of time writing long sections of prose as feedback to children about their work and covering the child's work with red pen, correcting every single error. Many teachers do this out of a sense of duty, but they are only too aware of the fact that the impact of the marking comments on the child's further work is minimal. The following questions need to be asked:

1 *Can children read your marking comments?*

2 *Can they understand your marking comments?*

3 *Do you allow time for them to read your marking comments?*

4 *Do you allow time for some improvement on the work to be made before moving on to the next activity, **or do you expect the child to be able to transfer your improvement suggestions to another piece of work in a new context?***

Even if the answer is positive for the first three questions, unless time is given for specific improvement on the work marked, marking becomes little more than a token exercise, and pieces of work generated one after the other, without any reflective thinking about how they could be improved. As Black and Wiliam (1998) found,

❛ *For assessment to be formative the feedback information has to be used.* ❜

The following issues about feedback to children have emerged from my work with teachers.

Feedback needs:

- **to be based on clear learning intentions/success criteria**

- **to take account of pupil self-evaluation**

- **to highlight where success occurred and where improvement could take place**

- **to be in a form which is accessible to the learner**

- **to give strategies for improvement (often oral), if this is beyond the means of the learner**

- **allocated time in which to take place or be read**

■ some focused improvement, based on the feedback, to take place.

Practical strategies

Drafting is a very supportive process for enabling improvement to take place from a starting point, but it is often only certain pieces of English work which get the benefit of this process.

Effective feedback goes into detail, making explicit where success was achieved and where improvements could be made. General comments such as *'Quite well achieved'* or *'mostly good adjectives used'* fall into the type of marking which provides an assessment record against learning intentions, but they do not provide useful feedback to the child. However, in order to give detailed feedback, there appears to be no alternative but to write a paragraph of text. With many pieces of work, the solution to this problem can be to create a simple coding system which is used to reflect the criteria of the learning intention. The following example shows how this can work:

Learning intention 1: To write a story showing two people's feelings from different points of view
Learning intention 2 (on second read through): to check spellings and punctuation

Activity: Discussion with the children about any two animals which are natural enemies, some kind of quest, chase or adventure which happens to them both and how they might both feel at each step of the story. The children then write their first draft, with the main focus being to show the feelings of the two creatures.

Ideal written marking comment, but will take a great deal of the teacher's time:

When you described the dog first setting eyes on the rabbit, you really described the dog's feelings well. Your use of the words 'trembling like a leaf', 'terrified' and 'not daring to breathe' were excellent ways of showing how frightened the

> *rabbit was when it thought the dog might find it's hiding place . . . etc, etc. However, when the dog lost the rabbit you could have said more about how frustrated he felt and also when the rabbit finally managed to escape . . . etc, etc.*

Although lengthy, it is clear that the child needs to know exactly what was successful and where improvements could be made. However, will the child be able to understand and follow your suggestions?

With a coding system, the same things are communicated to the child, but in a much simpler way. The children are told first *how* the piece will be marked. For instance:

> *'I will choose three places where you have successfully made me feel how that character was feeling and circle or highlight those bits. I will also choose one place where you could have said more about how one of the characters was feeling and I will put an arrow to show where you could have written more. I will also show spelling corrections by underlining words which are wrongly spelt.*

The marked work will now consist of only a few marks on the paper, indicating very clearly successes and improvement needs. Not only does this approach cut marking time considerably, it also, more importantly for feedback, gives highly accessible information to the child, requiring no reading or interpretation of remarks. If these codes worked for any learning intention, it would clearly be wise to use them throughout the school, but it needs to be remembered that the highlighting and arrow codes (or whatever is used) are not codes to denote secretarial skills, such as spelling errors or punctuation marks. So, in a piece of work where the learning intention was to use good adjectives, for example, the codes might underline three very good adjectives and place arrows under one or two words which could have been better described. Feedback

Success and improvement codes which reflect the learning intention/s

from teachers indicates that using codes which reflect the learning intention are useful in many contexts but mainly for English writing, and need to be used according to their appropriateness rather than as a blanket rule for everything.

The main issue here is how much the child is asked to focus on at once, beginning at the sharing learning intentions stage and moving on to marking and feedback. If children are asked to focus on fewer aspects of their work, thus maximising effort and concentration on that skill or concept, and if the subsequent feedback reflects those aims, the child is more likely to reach a higher standard of achievement.

Making time for improvement

After spending time on the lesson and then the marking, finding time for the child to consolidate and use this feedback seems vital, but because codes are so accessible, this time can be quite short and targeted. Either there and then, if the work was marked with the child, or, at the beginning of the next lesson if it was not, children can be asked to spend say no more than three minutes reading their underlined successful sections and be encouraged to feel proud of these successes. This could be done silently or in pairs, aloud to each other.

The children could then be asked to look at the arrowed section and to then think of a better way they could have described the person's feelings, or think of a better adjective, etc, etc. This can be done by pairs of children taking turns working together on each other's work orally, or children could simply write their new word or words at the end of their work. Obviously, this could not be done for every task, but where it is planned for, it will be extremely worthwhile in taking children forward with their development of a particular skill or concept.

This way of marking implies that aspects of writing which might have always been marked, such as spelling, grammar and punctuation, if not included as one of the learning intentions of the task, are not marked for that work or are only marked after a second draft, so that the first marking is limited and focused on one or two aspects only. When children are, occasionally, asked to focus on all aspects at once, we are creating a test situation. This is important from time to time, but unwieldy and unproductive for every task, because the child is having to consider too many criteria at once. The teacher falls into the role of copy editor, marking every error, rather than constructing useful feedback.

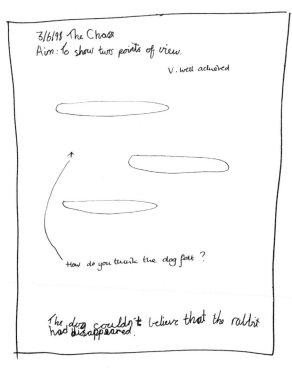

3/6/98 The Chase
Aim: to show two points of view.

V. well achieved

How do you think the dog felt?

The dog couldn't believe that the rabbit had disappeared.

One aspect improved by the child

How a piece of work might look, after marking and consolidation of feedback:

Date	**Title**
Learning Intentions:	**General comment**
(written by child if able)	*(written by teacher)*

Coded or marked work depending on appropriateness, focusing on limited aspects at a time

Child's self-evaluation comment (*if able*)

Comment including the words of the learning intention, if child unable to write fluently

Personal remarks to child regarding effort

Possibly: Child's attempt at improving the marked work

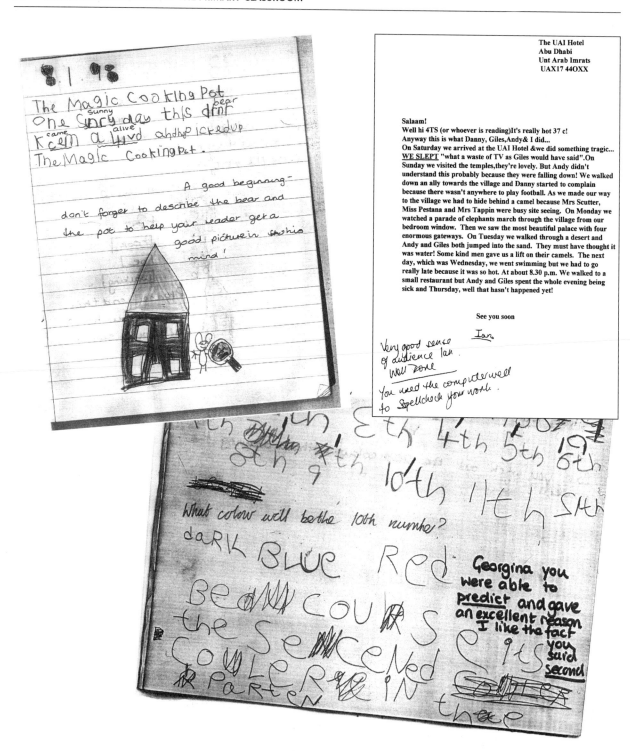

Examples of marked work including the learning intention in the teacher's comment and some targets

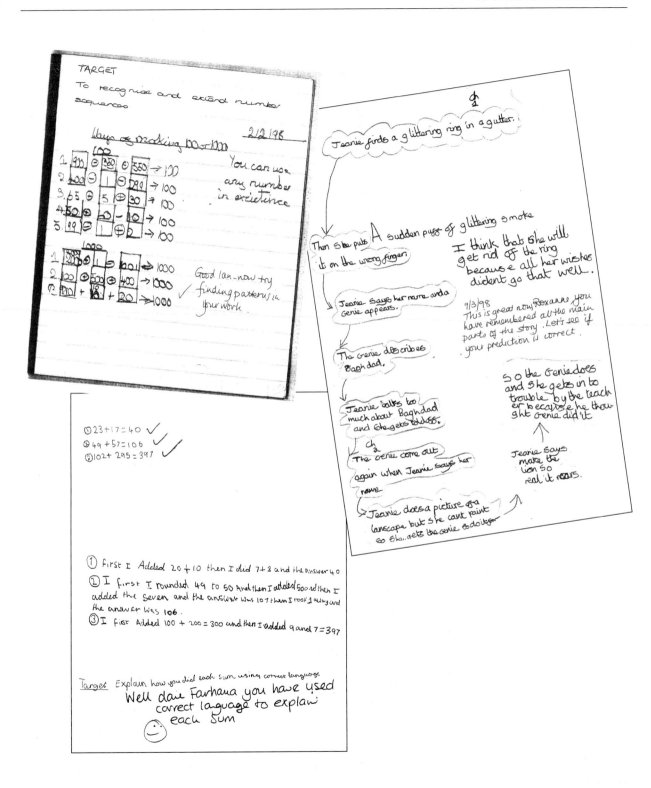

TARGET

To recognise and extend number sequences

Ways of making 100→1000

2/2/98

You can use any number in existence

Good Ian — now try finding patterns in your work ✓

---

① 23 + 17 = 40 ✓
② 49 + 57 = 106 ✓ ✓
③ 102 + 295 = 397 ✓

① First I *Added* 20 + 10 then I did 7 + 3 and the answer 40

② I First I rounded 49 to 50 And then I added 500 rd then I added the seven and the answer was 107 then I took 1 away and the answer was 106.

③ I first Added 100 + 200 = 300 and then I added 9 and 7 = 397

Target Explain how you did each sum using correct language

Well done Farhana you have used correct language to explain each sum ☺

Jeanie finds a glittering ring in a gutter.

Then She puts it on the wrong finger

A sudden puff of glittering smoke

I think that She will get rid of the ring because all her wishes didn't go that well.

Jeanie says her name and a Genie appears.

The Genie describes Baghdad.

Jeanie talks too much about Baghdad and She gets told off.

9/3/98
This is great now Roxanne you have remembered all the main parts of the story. Let's see if your prediction is correct.

So the Genie does and She gets into trouble by the teacher because he thought Genie did it

ch 2
The Genie come out again when Jeanie says her name

Jeanie Says make the lion so real it roars.

Jeanie does a picture of a landscape but she can't paint so She gets the Genie to do it for

The child's role in marking

After the first learning intention has been dealt with, children often pick up many of the mistakes which would otherwise involve the teacher in a period of unnecessary marking, if invited to check spelling and punctuation errors before the teacher marks the work. The process of children reconsidering their work in this way is part of their learning, so needs to be encouraged as a natural aspect of the school marking policy.

Where work is **marked with the child** it seems important to validate this in some way, by, for instance, writing 'Marked with child – discussed x, y and z'. This then not only explains the possible lack of marks on the piece by the teacher but reinforces the value of the teacher marking alongside the child, where the dialogue can be geared specifically to the needs of the individual.

Many schools have introduced paired or partnership oral marking, where children choose a suitable partner to discuss their work with or invite children to comment on their work in a group. The work done by Dorothy Grange (Northumberland advisory teacher) is well known in that area for the successes teachers have had with children using 'response partners'. For this role to impact on learning the following points are important:

■ *Success criteria/learning intentions are essential or the children will simply talk about neatness and punctuation.*

■ *One-to-one response partner work cannot be used until children have had experience in larger groups with teacher control.*

■ *It is essential for the class to identify the role of a response partner (or the success criteria for being a good response partner) through teacher role play.*

Example: Years 5/6

A response partner is someone who:

- talks about my work against the success criteria
- makes me feel good about my work because he/she points out what I have done well
- tells me how I could improve my work.

Example: Years 2/3

A response partner is someone who:

- helps me with my work
- tells the truth about my work
- helps me to make my work better.

To do this I need the teacher to tell me:

- the learning objectives
- the success criteria.

Marking in the Early Years

Many activities in the Early Years are practical, with no product capable of being marked. Nursery teachers traditionally write notes about children's development which feeds into their planning. However, it is possible to create a vehicle for 'marking' as well as other things which lie in the hands of the child. Many schools have 'practical' books for each child, which provide a vehicle for a number of processes, including marking. The book is organised as follows:

1   Each child has a 'Practical Book' (an A4 landscape plain paper exercise book), kept somewhere accessible.

2   Whenever children are involved in a structured practical activity (e.g. sand and water/construction material) they get/are given their practical book, which they keep near them.

3   For each child, the teacher writes, in advance, the date and the activity at the top of the page.

4   The space on the page is used in one of the following ways:

■ *It is left blank.*

■ The child uses the space for the last few minutes of the session to *'put down on paper what you were doing to show someone who was not there'* – the equivalent of emergent writing, giving interesting insights about the child's perceptions and very often what they are capable of which has not been previously revealed (see examples below).

■ The child uses the space for any 'jottings' which occur naturally during the activity, which are commonly put on scrap paper and then thrown away – this ensures that the children's marks are kept in one place.

■ The space is used as a place for *a comment by the teacher* for significant achievement. The comment is written to the child and the child is told what is being written. Although the child may not be able to read the comment, it will still have an impact and is likely to be remembered by the child.

The 'Practical Book' has been a very popular initiative in many schools, giving greater value to practical activities. Even if the book consisted of nothing but the teacher's description of each practical activity, this alone is a valuable record of every structured practical task the child has been involved in; a bonus for parents' evenings when teachers are often pressed to have something to 'show' for all the work which has been done during the year.

The book also encourages good practice for children in recording a reflection of what they have done, especially for mathematics. Followed through the age ranges, a mathematics exercise book by Year 6, for example, would have a date and title for every maths activity (this time written by the child, of course) with either the work itself or a reflective short account/evaluation for practical activities such as games or problems. Children need to be able to first orally express, then write notes about their thinking processes and steps taken in a practical task for mathematics, mirroring the way children are commonly asked to write accounts of scientific investigations.

The marking policy

Marking policies are usually either embedded in the assessment policy or stand alone and are referred to in the assessment policy. The following section from *Teacher Assessment in Key Stage 2* helpfully summarises the issues and principles involved:

Pages from a child's 'Practical Book'

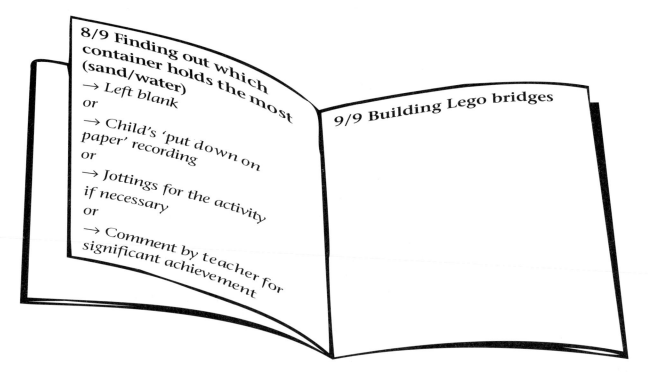

8/9 Finding out which container holds the most (sand/water)

→ Left blank
or

→ Child's 'put down on paper' recording
or

→ Jottings for the activity if necessary
or

→ Comment by teacher for significant achievement

9/9 Building Lego bridges

6 *Effective marking can:*

- *provide clear feedback to children about strengths and weaknesses in their work;*

- *recognise, encourage and reward children's effort and progress;*

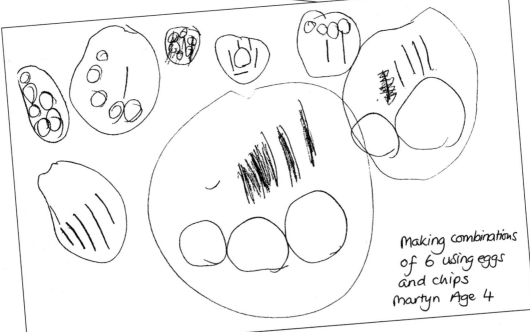

Examples of children's early recording after practical activity

Examples of children's early recording after practical activity

■ *focus teachers on those areas of learning where groups and individual children need specific help;*

■ *provide a record of children's progress; and*

■ *help parents understand strengths and weaknesses in children's work.*

When marking children's work, teachers need to consider whether:

■ *comments are to form the basis of a discussion between teacher and child;*

■ *children are expected to read comments;*

■ *comments are to inform future work; and/or*

■ *comments are to correct or improve an existing piece of work.*

There is a wide variety in practice in marking. Many schools find it helpful to devise guidelines for teachers to support consistency in their marking and also specify who monitors the quality of teachers' marking. These guidelines could include the principles below.

Comments on children's work should:

■ *relate to planned learning objectives;*

■ *be legible and clear in meaning;*

■ *recognise children's achievements; and*

■ *indicate the next steps in children's learning.*

Time needs to be built into lessons for children to reflect on marking and respond to it. ❥

(SCAA 1997)

4 Target setting

Target setting is a multi-layered concept which has become the vehicle for 'improving standards'. Broadly speaking, the basic principle of target setting is to use a set of process steps in order to identify weaknesses, target aims for future improvement then set out to meet the aims.

Target setting is multi-layered because it has been established at the following levels: national, LEA, school, class and pupil, with national targets filtering down to pupil level.

How it all works

1   The Government has announced national targets for literacy and numeracy requiring that, by the year 2002:

  ■ **80 per cent of 11-year-olds will reach Level 4 in English; and**

  ■ **75 per cent of 11-year-olds will reach Level 4 in mathematics**

2   LEAs, in order to meet the national targets, have been allocated the percentage of Level 4s, overall, which they should meet. This therefore means that each LEA's targets will depend on the particular context of the LEA.

3   LEAs then set out the percentage of Level 4s that each school should strive for, depending on the context of each individual school.

4   Each school goes through the same process, deciding what each class should aim for.

5   Finally, the class teacher sets targets for individual children. Although end of Key Stage teachers might set targets in the form of the number of Level 3s or 4s to be attained, pupil target setting is mainly concerned with learning targets, rather than numbers.

The DFEE, QCA and OFSTED outlined the process steps for target setting at the school level as follows:

Stage 1   analyses its current performance:
           'How well are we doing?'

           Looking critically at pupils' current achievements is an essential first step towards improvement.

Stage 2   compares its results with those of similar schools:
           'How well should we be doing?'

           By comparing current and previous results, and those from similar schools, a school can better judge performance.

Stage 3   sets itself clear and measurable targets:
           'What more can we aim to achieve?'

           With good information, a school can set itself realistic and challenging targets for improvement.

Stage 4   revises its development plan to highlight action to achieve the targets:
           'What must we do to make it happen?'
           Once it has set its targets, the school must then take determined action to improve.

Stage 5   takes action, reviews success, and starts the cycle again.

           A school must monitor and evaluate its actions in terms of improved pupil performance.

                                (DFEE *From Targets to Action*, 1997)

They go on to say:

6   *Of course, targets alone will not raise standards in schools. They are the next step in improving development planning. They need to fit into a sensible cycle of school review,*

planning and action. They are a further management tool which head teachers and governing bodies can use. "
(DFEE 1997)

It is important that teachers hang on to these words, for it seems to be in direct conflict with a system which demands, rather than hopes for, a greater number of children attaining above average levels than would be expected.

The obvious dilemma about the current interpretation of target setting, is that, while we must approve the desire to improve standards, we run into a number of difficulties when we make the measure of improvement simply the number of Level 4s a school has attained.

Firstly, according to well-established research, any 'high stakes' testing (testing where the results matter) inevitably leads to a narrowing of the curriculum and 'teaching to the test' because teachers want their children to do as well as they can on the test (Airasian 1988). This often means that the curriculum is focused on 'surface' rather than 'deep' learning (Harlen and James 1997). With the added pressure on schools to achieve a greater number of high levels, the situation is compounded.

Secondly, common advice given to schools is to 'target' individual children in a class who stand the greatest chance of moving from one level to another, so that they would receive more focused teaching than other children in order to bring up the number of high levels. In terms of equal opportunities for all pupils this seems to be an outrageous suggestion, but it appears to be inevitable if schools are pressured into attaining the desired results. David Jesson (University of Sheffield) gives an alternative suggestion that we should instead be targeting *underachievement at all levels*. In other words, if individual children are to receive more attention than others in the class, which is debatable, it should be those children who are underachieving according to their ability, which would span across the ability range.

Thirdly, defining improvement as the extent to which children performed successfully at an external test assumes that the test was valid and reliable and did not advantage or disadvantage particular pupils according to race, gender, class or any other factor. When so much is at stake for a school, it is vital that these issues are addressed by test constructors and evaluators. It also assumes that the tests have remained constant and unchanging in their level of difficulty and in their basic demands. This has certainly not been the case so far since the introduction of the National Curriculum's associated testing. Year on year comparisons can only provide valuable information if there has been a period of stability. However, to a certain extent, maybe we need to accept that there will be some changes each year, or comparisons will never be able to be made. Where comparisons seem surprising, the extent to which the changes affected them could be considered.

The process steps provided by the DFEE are, in themselves, an excellent framework for effecting change. However, there are certain factors which can make or break the extent to which success can be achieved. As already stated, setting targets does not, in itself, raise standards. Before the targets have been set, the school needs to be able to correctly identify weaknesses, whether within the context of an under achieving, average or high achieving school. In terms of low test results, this can be fairly straightforward, once value-added factors have been used to ensure that there really are weaknesses.

At 'Stage 2' the school *compares its results with those of similar schools'*. This can be extremely useful in confirming expectations or challenging them, but again, there are several possible hazards. If the schools are broadly similar in not only their intake but in the story of the school (stability of staff, level of resourcing and so on), comparisons can highlight possible discrepancies in results which can then lead to analysis and action. However, attempting to find out what the better school is doing which the other school is not is fraught with difficulties. It might be that there are several obvious factors which could be gleaned from seeing copies of planning and assessment systems, but it is unlikely that simply visiting a school would unearth all the subtleties of success, which might be contributed to the leadership of the head or senior managers, the relationships between staff or the quality of several gifted teachers, amongst many possible factors. Comparing results in a fairly general way and seeing the contact with other schools as a vehicle for dialogue and exchange of ideas is likely to be more helpful as a starting point for probing and analysing a school's results.

The next stage is even more critical. The school must then decide what it must do to improve things. It is unlikely that a school will know what needs to be included in specific targets (broad targets such as *'improve children's reading ability'* are easy), because, presumably, if they had known what was needed, they would have already done it. The school therefore needs external support, probably in the form of INSET or other training, so that strategies for improvement can be outlined and understood. The extent to which the school can use external agencies depends on its particular financial situation and the availability of LEA advisory staff. Without the 'how to' stage being supported, it is possible for a school to set vague targets, go about improvements in ways which are ineffective and then face demoralisation at the lack of improvement. *Excellence in Schools* (the 1997 White Paper) takes account of the importance of support during the process of target setting by placing this responsibility firmly in the hands of the LEA. Roles are defined in the following way:

> *Each school sets draft targets, taking account of the comparative data and their own previous best performance, for discussion with its LEA.*
>
> *Schools and LEAs agree targets, covering a 3 year period and subject to annual review.*
>
> *Where exceptionally an LEA cannot reach agreement with a school on its targets, the LEA may invoke the early warning system . . .*

The LEA plays a key role, then, although the White Paper continues:

> *The role of LEAs is not to control schools, but to challenge all schools to improve and support those which need help to raise standards.*
>
> (*Excellence in Schools*, 1997)

In the drive for ever higher standards, it is important to consider the impact of increased expectation on both pupils and teachers. People can only take steps forward if their self-esteem is high and they are confident in their ability to improve. Barber's diagram shows the relationship between teacher expectation and self-esteem:

SELF-ESTEEM

		Low	High
EXPECTATIONS	Low	Failure	Complacency
	High	Demoralisation	Success

(Barber 1996)

The worrying area of the table is where low self-esteem meets high teacher expectation, with its resulting 'demoralisation', often leading to opting out by the time a child is of secondary age. Many teachers, as well as pupils, might feel that they have been continually pressed to do better without any regard being paid to their self-esteem. Clearly there are lessons to be learnt here: raising expectations must go hand in hand with raising self-esteem.

Target setting at school level

Using the test results as a starting point for identifying strengths and weaknesses in the school can be very useful in setting targets for school improvement. As long as the statutory data allows you to see results for each question, it is possible to isolate those areas of the tested curriculum in which the year group appeared to underachieve. We might, for instance, notice that area, multiplication and understanding of decimals questions were clear areas of weakness in the tests. As long as you are satisfied that the test questions were valid (i.e. the question tested exactly what it was supposed to test), the weak area can be the target for school improvement, because it probably points to a general weakness in the school's mathematics policy and mathematics teaching.

These targets are essentially planning and staff development issues rather than a vehicle for individual target setting. Ways of tackling the targeted aspects might include, for instance, finding ways of improving the mathematics scheme of work, monitoring and supporting the teaching in classrooms and planning a programme of inservice training.

Target setting at class level

Although very simplistic, a strategy for stating expectations explicitly is to decide, after baseline assessment, and/or at the end of Year 2 (after the Key Stage 1 test and Teacher Assessment results have been finalised), the predicted level for each child for the core subject Attainment Targets by the end of Year 6. A child achieving Level 2c for reading in the Key Stage 1 test, for example, might be predicted to be able to reach Level 3, or possibly Level 4. A Level 3a, similarly, is likely to have Level 5 set as the target for reading by the end of Year 6.

These predictions can then be monitored at the end of each year by each teacher, deciding whether each child is 'on track' or not, and whether appropriate action should take place.

This approach is merely a vehicle for ensuring consistency in expectations through several years, ensuring that the change of teachers does not divert attention from the initial projection for each child.

Target setting at pupil level

Individual target setting seems to make most sense if it is based on and works upwards from the child's actual achievement rather than downwards from school or higher level targets (although class targets, of course, frame the overall direction for the child). In order to raise achievement for all children in the class, we need to set learning targets for every child. This might seem a daunting prospect, but the key to its manageability is likely to be in the design of the system. The following strategy appears to make target setting a manageable task and has many positive spin-offs:

Target cards

Each child has a 'Writing Target card', consisting of an index card. This is kept either in an envelope on a display board with the name of the child on the flap of the envelope or in a box in the centre of each table.

Children collect or take out their writing target cards every time they do any writing, for any subject and keep it beside them on their desk. Alternatively, the cards are kept in the back of the child's writing book and only used when that book is being used, in order to limit the focus.

A target card might look like this:

> **9/9 Try not to reverse your bs and ds ✓**
>
> **21/9 Try to use then and but in your stories ✓**
>
> **20/10 Try to use your word book less often, and have a go at the words ✓**
>
> **26/10 Make sure that you don't waste time at the beginning of your writing**

The targets can be defined as **the next most achievable target** in the development of that child's writing. The target is deliberately one which the child is close to achieving, or would be able to achieve in approximately the next three weeks and which, with a sharper focus, will be achieved sooner. Achievable targets enable children to increase the pace of improvement and increase motivation and self-esteem. Targets which are too far away from actual performance do the reverse. They are often less clearly defined (because the teacher cannot pinpoint the exact needs of the child) and run the risk of being unachievable, therefore demotivating the child. Of course, teachers need clear targets for a child's development throughout the year, but these are specified in the Programmes of Study, in schools' schemes of work. They manifest themselves in teachers' planning formats and materialise in short-term plans as a result of assessment judgements (e.g. Joe, Mia and Rebecca need more challenging place value activities tomorrow).

Writing the targets on cards means they are constantly visible, both to the teacher and the child. Targets written in exercise books disappear as soon as the child turns the page, and both child and teacher forget the target. With this system, when children finish their work they give in the card with the writing (slipped in the book, attached to paper with a paper clip or both paper and card slipped into a plastic A4 wallet . . .) and the target is taken account of when marking, as well as the extent to which the learning intentions of the task have been met.

It might seem that the child is being given another learning intention to deal with, but the focus on the target is essentially different. Learning intentions are the focus of one lesson, whereas writing targets are ongoing, threading through all aspects of writing and possible home experiences. Feedback from teachers suggests that this system is highly manageable and has an immediately positive impact on children's writing and their motivation. Many teachers have reported on quite significant improvement in children's achievement as a result of the target cards, and a keen interest developing from parents, as the child communicates the targets at home. Although the teacher sets the first target, children are encouraged to set targets as their awareness of their achievement increases. If children are being encouraged to be self-evaluative and comment on their learning, making suggestions for targets and identifying when they have been achieved will pose no problems.

Teachers sometimes worry that they might not 'get the target right' and the child will face defeat. If this happens, a new target should be negotiated with the child, leaving the old target to be dated at a later date.

Similarly, what do you do if a child appears to regress? The fact that the target was achieved in the first instance should not be undermined. A new target should be set which extends the original target (e.g. *'Try not to reverse your bs and ds in 10 consecutive pieces of work'*).

DATE SET	TARGET	DATE ACHIEVED
Jan 98	To write his name independently	can write D, a; March98
Jan 98	– To retell his book in his own words.	starting to go into more detail March 98
	– To improve pencil control. – threading, plastic Lego.	– holds pencil when reminded
March 98	– To make representational drawings.	
March 98	– To sit on the carpet without calling out	

Rabby

- Remember to write in sentences. Each sentence must have a capital letter and a full STOP. 17.

- **When you write, read your work and check that you have put in all the words.** 7·1·98

- Use a <u>dictionary</u> to check how to spell words that you are not sure of. 12·1·98

- When you have a go at spelling listen to the <u>end</u> of the word. ✓ 23·9

- When you spell a new word listen to the <u>vowels</u> you can hear. a – e – i – o – u .

DATE SET	TARGET	DATE ACHIEVED
JAN '98	To listen to instructions first time.	
	To be able to work more quickly when writing.	16·3·98
27·1·98	To write in sentences when answering comprehension questions	9·2·98
"	Able to tell the difference between fiction + non-fiction	27·1·98
16·3·98	To be able to complete a piece of work within a specified time.	

Examples of target cards

DATE SET	TARGET	DATE ACHIEVED
7/9.	To know her nos to 10.	✓
10/10	Read, write + order read write order nos-20	3/3/98
I EP	To know her number bonds to 10	with apparatus does not know them off by heart.
5/11	To be able to add to 15	with support 11/2.
26/11	To be able to subtract to 15	
23/2	To recognise a metre stick	✓
24/2	To know that we measure length in cm\m	3/3
10/3.	To be able to tell the time on the hour.	

10.2.98.
put 5 interesting adjectives into a story.

16.10.97
Use commers when listing

10.98
Learn to write a story or factual piece in paragraphs

11.3.98
Proof read for punctuation.

12.3.98
Proof read for spellings.

1.4.98
Use a dictionary to check the

spellings in all your written work for one day.

3.4.98
Write a story or factual piece using paragraphs and check all punct

Examples of target cards

How many target cards should there be?

It seems manageable to have three sets of targets at once: for writing, numeracy (or mathematics) and reading, with reading perhaps not written on cards. The mathematics target cards would be set up in the same way as the writing cards, with targets spanning the range of achievement (attitude, use of resources, social factors, recording as well as points about the mathematics itself). Because, traditionally, teachers feel less confident about mathematics, it would be useful to have staff meetings where teachers see each other's target cards and compare the types of targets they are setting. The targets set will, to some extent, reflect the teacher's understanding of mathematics teaching.

Reading targets could be written on children's individual reading records when the teacher is hearing the child read, and presented to the child orally. As an alternative strategy, some schools have created reading target cards in the form of book marks, to make them more visible to children.

In Nursery and Reception, teachers trialling target cards for social development only have given positive feedback about their impact. Targets are often pictorial and are communicated orally.

Managing the targets

The only time all targets need to be written at once is when the teacher creates the cards and writes the first targets. Thereafter, new targets will be staggered, because children will be meeting them at different times. For younger children, or children with reading difficulties, it is necessary to make clear what the new target says, although the target will often be created alongside the child anyway. Children are highly motivated by their targets, and appear to remember them very quickly, even if they cannot read them, probably because they are very personal and clearly belong to them. Children become increasingly more able to say what they think their next target should be and when they believe they have fulfilled a target, thus decreasing the workload for the teacher and shifting more of the responsibility for learning into the hands of the child.

The spin-offs

By the end of the year, each child has a set of target cards, stored by the teacher, which provide invaluable information, both for end of year report writing and for the receiving teacher. The last card is passed up to the next teacher who continues to use it with the existing ongoing target. This ensures continuity for the child and the teacher, making sure that no time is wasted finding out what the child needs to do next.

The cards provide evidence of targets which focus on the child's writing development across the full range of achievement (social, physical and attitude targets might feature, as well as concepts and processes), thus maximising the chances of improved achievement.

Several teachers have commented that the target cards enable the teacher to identify underachievement for more able children, because these children are, perhaps, more complacent.

The most important impact of setting targets, of course, is that children's increased motivation, perseverance and involvement in their own development and progress are further factors leading to higher levels of self-esteem and academic achievement.

5 The Record of Achievement: celebrating achievement of 'whole child' development

Every teacher knows that children's educational development depends on much more than their ability to fulfil academic learning intentions. Indeed, research indicates that there is a definite link between so-called 'non-academic' achievement, if celebrated and used to raise pupil self-esteem, having an impact on a child's academic achievement. This means that we cannot afford to marginalise achievement which is not directly related to our lesson plans.

My previous work with teachers led us to believe that children's achievement falls into five categories (Clarke 1996):

■ physical achievement

■ social achievement

■ attitude development

■ conceptual achievement

■ process skill achievement.

What seems to be important is that the five categories are *treated in the same way* by the teacher when the child achieves success, so that we communicate the message that *all of these aspects of achievement are academic* and have equal weight in contributing to ultimate academic achievement. It is common for children to encounter different treatment of the five areas, such as gold stars or assembly certificates for good behaviour, social or physical achievement, but great praise from the teacher for conceptual or process achievement via marking, verbal comments and possible placing of examples of work in a pupil portfolio or Record of Achievement. Thus, the practice in the classroom can, without us realising, reinforce the notion that physical, social and attitude achievement is unrelated to academic achievement. I believe that children know very well that what really counts is conceptual and process achievement (the limited definition of academic achievement), no matter how many gold stars they receive for other things.

If we acknowledge the links between social, physical and attitude development with academic improvement, we are actually redefining **all of these** as 'academic achievement', rather than 'non-academic' and 'academic' achievement. Communicating this to children seems vital, so that, for instance, a child who learns how to throw a ball or listen during story time will understand that these achievements will affect and improve their reading, writing and other abilities.

At the heart of the idea of achievement is the importance of high self-esteem as a necessary factor for successful learning. Barber's chart on p. 90 is relevant again in demonstrating that we need to balance high teach expectation with strategies for developing children's self-esteem. Without this link, children become demoralised, underachieve or fail. Various studies carried out in the last ten years have shown that low achievers tend to attribute failure to low ability and higher achievers tend to attribute success to the amount of effort put in. Vispoel and Austin (1995) advised teachers to try to change this perception by encouraging children to view learning as a continuum which, given time, anyone can master.

The Record of Achievement can be a vehicle for reinforcing the equality of different types of achievement, *as long as the record contains or refers to examples of both products and events for all aspects of achievement. Achievement is defined as something either the child or teacher is proud of or thinks is significant.*

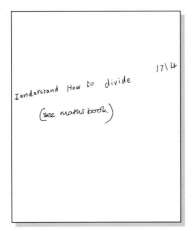

Reference sheets showing achievement for which there is no end-product

Some practical strategies for enabling this to happen:

First possibility

■ Create blank record sheets (certificates) on which important social, physical or attitude achievements can be written by either teacher or child (e.g. Joe swam 50 metres today/I can now sit quietly in the reading corner/Mia has stopped panicking when she has to do some writing) and then placed into the child's Record of Achievement (using folders, concertina files or plastic page books) along with products. Alternatively, the Record of Achievement could contain only these record sheets, each referring to either event achievement or product achievement which can be found in a child's book.

Second possibility

■ Give each child an exercise book (e.g. **My Achievement book**) in which entries are written, either by teacher or child, for any kind of achievement, such as '**2/9/99 Karim published an excellent book on Victorian buildings**'/**1/6/98 I have learnt my ×8 tables**/**13/4/98 I can understand decimals**. No work is stored, because it can all be found from the references in the Achievement book. This system is extremely manageable.

Achievements entered in an Achievement Book by teacher and/or child

Using the Record of Achievement

There have been times when the term *Record of Achievement* or *Pupil Profile* referred to a device which attempted to provide a rigorous track of progress in the National Curriculum. The aim of these documents was to have a set number of annotated examples of English, mathematics and science works. Its usefulness and manageability was often debated.

If there are clear practices in the school for ensuring that the full range of formative assessment strategies are being used (i.e. planning, assessment notes in short-term planning, sharing learning intentions, pupil self-evaluation, marking against learning intentions and target setting), the Record of Achievement does not have to provide a rigorous progress record against the National Curriculum, as these strategies already perform that function. Instead, it can be a celebration of achievement, with its main purpose to raise self-esteem, motivate children and encourage them to recognise their abilities and progress. Although it would be important to make sure that all children had things in their Record, the content for each child is likely to be quite different.

The rationale for the Record of Achievement needs to be explained to children so that they realise that all kinds of achievement (physical, social, etc) will be valued equally. Anything either kept or recorded could be **significant** for that child (i.e. the teacher feels that the achievement is important enough to be written down and could consist of a relatively small achievement) or is achievement which the child/teacher is particularly pleased with (this allows for children who continually do well to be equally treated and relieves the teacher from always looking for 'significance').

It seems to work best if teachers look out for good achievement and children are asked to say when they think they have done or achieved something they are proud of (for any aspect of achievement). The teacher has the final say and then the achievement is noted either by the teacher or the child using one of the above systems.

An alternative or additional, more structured, approach is to ask children, at the end of the week or month, to choose anything from the week/month which they would like either placed or written about (product or event) for their Record of Achievement. To avoid lots of photocopying, reference slips to products can be written, saying where they could be found (e.g. *'Problem solving about mazes in maths book 16/3'*). If the **Achievement book** is used, where achievement is simply entered without storing the work, the child or teacher enters the achievement. This approach builds entirely on the previous processes dealt with in this book and would be difficult to achieve if children were not continually considering learning intentions and self-evaluating. In fact, by the end of the week, children should have a good idea of what they will choose as their entry. This more structured, reflective approach means that the teacher is not having to be so aware of making sure that children do not 'fall through the net'. A combination of both approaches would perhaps be the ideal situation.

The previous chapters of this book have clear links with the Record of Achievement. If children are used to self-evaluation, they will be much more likely to be able to determine their own achievements for the Record. Marking could indicate when a piece of work shows some important achievement and that it could go into the Record. Similarly, as individual targets are met, these can also be referenced and placed in the Record of Achievement.

At the end of the Year, it is common practice for a few pieces from the Record of Achievement to be passed up to the next teacher and the rest of the contents to be sent home with the child, having achieved their formative purpose throughout the year.

6 Summative assessment and its uses

This final chapter takes various aspects of summative assessment in turn, establishing definitions and purposes and practical strategies for effective use, if that is relevant. Many technical books and articles have been written about these areas of assessment, so I am attempting only to provide summary information and practical advice.

Baseline assessment

Baseline assessment became statutory in September 1998. QCA accredited a large number of baseline schemes, both commercially produced and LEA-based, giving schools a choice.

The purpose of baseline assessment is to assess children on entry to school, establishing their abilities before their education has become the responsibility of the school. There are two basic functions of baseline testing:

1 *Diagnostic:* to highlight individual strengths and weaknesses, so that children's needs can be met from the earliest possible point.

2 *Measuring progress:* to establish a baseline on which later information can be built, thus contextualising achievement by showing how much actual progress has been made.

Diagnostic uses

The AAIA (Assessment Advisors and Inspectors Association) advice on choosing or developing a baseline scheme lists a number of diagnostic purposes.

❝ *An effective baseline scheme should:*

- *be formative, supporting teaching and learning for individual children*

- *establish children's starting points, i.e. what children know, understand and can do on entering compulsory education*

- *enable teachers to match the curriculum to the needs of children by indicating clear learning objectives*

- *contribute to the early identification of special educational needs and the needs of more able children*

- *support the introduction of children to the National Curriculum Programmes of Study, as and when appropriate*

- *provide a common framework for dialogue between all parties (teachers, support assistants and parents)*

- *support assessment which has high validity*

- *provide a structure for the development of consistency and reliability*

- *improve continuity and progression between home, pre-school provision and school.* ❞

(AAIA 1997)

There seems to be a central dilemma when choosing a baseline scheme: the classic conflict between validity and reliability, with manageability creating other concerns. Some schemes have rather open criteria which the teacher uses to make assessments (e.g. can read fluently/can work cooperatively). This approach means that all aspects of achievement can be assessed and the validity is high (what is intended to be assessed is assessed). However, the lack of clarity in the criteria means that teachers could interpret them differently, resulting in poor reliability. Baseline schemes which focus the criteria, on the other hand, can either limit the possibilities for assessment (possibly marginalising social and attitude development) or, by organising the criteria into booklets in which children draw, write or indicate pictures, the reliability is increased but validity can be questionable.

The best baseline schemes seem to be those which fall between the two approaches, perhaps stating the criteria for observations or dialogue, but giving a clear breakdown of examples of what this might mean in reality. The Surrey baseline scheme, for example, includes the following examples to help teachers decide attainment for the criterion:

To assess the pupil's ability to use a variety of grammatical structures and lengths of utterances

P1 Uses single words
The pupil uses simple single words to communicate, such as 'hello', 'no!'.

P2 Uses phrases
The pupil uses single words and some simple two-three word phrases, such as 'want swing'.

1 Uses simple sentences
The pupil is observed using some phrases and simple sentences (which may have grammatical errors, such as 'I go'ed on swings').

2 Uses sentences of more than five words
The pupil uses a variety of simple sentences and phrases, many with five or more words (which may occasionally have some grammatical error, e.g. 'Me go on the swings high up').

3 Uses extended sentences

The pupil is able to use extended sentences, in an interesting and logical way (although there may be some small errors in grammatical construction, such as 'My dad, Shep and me go high up on the swings in the park').

4 Uses complex sentences

The pupil is able to use complex sentences which include subordinate clauses and are usually grammatically correct, such as 'When my Dad and I went to the park with my dog Shep, I went really high on the swings.

(Surrey County Council)

The AAIA advice states that

an effective baseline scheme should:

- *be based upon observation, discussion and questioning as the main means of assessment, supported by tangible evidence where appropriate*

- *be unobtrusive to children*

- *utilise children's first language where at all possible*

- *allow the best possible access to all pupils*

- *support meaningful dialogue with parents/carers*

- *have assessment criteria which promote dialogue and sharing of good practice between early years staff and result in consistent interpretation of the assessment criteria*

- *support the development of shared learning objectives and help staff to plan more effectively*

- *not make unreasonable demands upon teachers' time or school budgets.*

(AAIA 1997)

The Baseline Assessment statements for **mathematics** are:

Code	Using and Applying Mathematics	Number (focus on counting)	Shape, Space and Measures (focus on shape)
O		*(See the description of the evaluative criteria on page 13)*	
A	Participates in classroom activities showing mathematical awareness	Counts with objects to 5	Begins to explore the mathematical properties of objects and shapes
B	Participates in classroom activities, and displays some mathematical understanding verbally	Recognises, counts with objects and orders numbers to at least 10	Works with 3D objects and 2D shapes and uses everyday language to display some understanding of their mathematical properties
C	Participates in structured and unstructured maths activities and begins to use familiar mathematical language	Recognises, counts and writes numbers to at least 20 with a reasonable degree of accuracy	Names common 3D objects and 2D shapes and describes their properties

Part of Birmingham LEA baseline scheme – mathematics

Mathematical Skills

4 Number Skills

① Can count up to five objects with 1:1 correspondence.
Counting familiar toys, bricks, counters placed in a line with approximately the same distance between them.

② Can add and subtract objects to a total of five.
Addition: place objects in two groups and ask how many there are altogether.
Subtraction: put out 3, 4 or 5 objects and say how many are left if 1, 2 or 3 are removed.

③ Can use number facts, including addition and subtraction, to a total of ten.
Has some number facts of addition or subtraction to totals of 10 without necessarily having to use objects and count on or count back for each operation.

Ⓝ None of the above.

5 Sequencing

① Can copy a short sequence (5-10) of beads or shapes.
If a short sequence of blocks, beads, Lego bricks, counters, etc, of different colours or shapes is placed in front of the child, he/she can copy the same sequence using the same kinds of materials.

② Can devise repeating patterns.
Using any of the above items, the child can construct his or her own repeating pattern.

③ Can complete number sentences to 10.
Can complete number sentences to ten of the form 2+3= (or similar).

Ⓝ None of the above.

6 Maths

① Follows instructions related to movement and position.
Follows instructions involving the language of movement (e.g. 'move it', 'place it' – under, over, next to, in front of, behind) using toys or bricks, counters, etc.

② Can use mathematical terms for common 2D shapes (e.g. square, circle, triangle, rectangle, diamond).

③ Can give instructions related to movement and position.
Can give adults instructions as in 1 above.

Ⓝ None of the above.

7 Sets and Graphs

① Can select a named object from an array of objects when requested verbally (e.g. a square from a set of shapes, a specified coloured object from an array of different coloured objects).
Given a set of 4–6 objects of different colours or shape, can select one using the appropriate criterion given by verbal instruction – 'give me a red one', or 'give me a square one'.

② Can sort a set of objects according to a specified criterion (by any one of colour, size or shape).
Given a group of objects, can sort them into 2 or 3 sets according to one specified criterion, e.g. colour or size or shape.

③ Can interpret simple bar charts.

Ⓝ None of the above.

*Part of **Baseline-plus *(Edexcel)* baseline scheme** – mathematics*

Measuring progress

This aspect of baseline assessment is in its early stages. The theory is that it should be possible to link up baseline scores with Key Stage 1 Assessment, then Key Stage 2, in order to show progression for the child and the effectiveness of the school. The feasibility of being able to do this accurately is in question, because the same test is not being used at each stage. As the tests are different, progress can only be measured in a relatively loose way, picking up test items which are related (e.g. both items test ability to count to 10). It seems, at this stage, that work carried out so far by universities attached to LEA baseline work has led to interesting information about useful indicators. For instance, if a child is good at rhyming at entry to school, they are more likely to be an above average reader by the end of Key Stage 1 (Surrey baseline work: Thomas *et al* 1997).

From a school perspective, the amount of progress made, in general terms, can be useful in monitoring the effectiveness of the teaching. If many children appear to have made little progress in particular aspects, it could be a useful starting point for identifying school targets for improvement. It would be important, however, through investigation, to establish the exact reasons for the lack of progress, in order to know whether it is possible to do anything about it. If, for instance, the problem lay in the hands of the teacher, some change could be effected, whereas if the problem had arisen because of the movement of children in the cohort, for instance, the situation would be beyond the control of the school.

Benchmarking

Benchmarking is the term given to the process of measuring standards of actual performance against those achieved by others with broadly similar characteristics, identifying what it is they are doing and learning from it in order to improve. QCA publishes data for schools using data from Key Stage 1 and 2 results in order to enable schools to engage in this exercise.

Again, we are in the early stages of this process becoming properly established, so what is written now is likely to become quickly out of date. However, the issues surrounding the idea of benchmarking, I believe, will not.

Although schools appear to be grateful to be able to compare their results with those of similar schools (out of curiosity and for confirmation of expectations), the concept of benchmarking, when applied to education, is plagued with problems, some similar to those outlined for target setting. The first issue is the criteria used for grouping schools. QCA is using prior attainment (baseline scores) and the proportion of children in the school taking free school meals and the proportion of children for whom English is an additional language. Although these characteristics might correlate with test scores, it does not necessarily mean that the schools are similar. Apart from unincluded aspects of the stated criteria, such as the number of children entitled to free school meals who do not claim them and the types of additional languages and corresponding adult support in the school, there are other, more subtle factors to consider.

Two 'similar' schools might have very different staffing characteristics, for instance, one (as is common in many inner city schools) having a high turnover of staff, including the headteacher, while the other might have a stable, well-established set-up. Movement of children, especially children with English as an additional language, service children and travellers, can dramatically affect the results in a school. I am sure these examples are representative of the tip of the iceberg. If schools are to actively find out what is happening in a more successful school, these are very real issues. However, even if the schools are indeed very similar, there remains the complex idea of the feasibility of being able to find out what another school is doing that you are not.

Key features of a successful school might consist of a multitude of things, ranging from easily identified factors such as the quality of schemes of work and planning systems to almost hidden aspects, such as the style of the head, the quality of the leadership, the relationship between the staff and the self-esteem of those working in the school. All these factors contribute to the well-being and achievement of the school. How long would it take to identify these factors so that they could be usefully transferred? Even then, would it actually be possible for a school to simply 'take on' systems without the appropriate INSET and monitoring, discussion and informal talk, all of which facilitate change and would be invisible when visiting the school, because they would have already happened?

Comparisons with other schools can, however, be used in a positive, albeit simplistic, way. If schools compare their test results with other schools they can see how their scores compare with other schools for each test, thus providing some help for schools in setting realistic targets for improvement. The following table, reproduced from the SCAA consultation paper *Target Setting and Benchmarking in Schools*, shows the kind of information schools are presented with:

	95 perc.		UQ		MED		LQ	
English								
TA	95		84	77	75		65	
Reading Test	94		82		73	68	63	
Writing Test	96		84	78	76		65	
Mathematics								
TA	98	92	88		80		70	
Test	98	93	88		80		70	
Science								
TA	100		91	85	82		72	

KSI results: schools with up to 50% of EAL pupils and 20–35% taking free school meals

% of pupils achieving level 2 and above
Table 'exploded' to allow schools to plot their own results.

The chart shows, for instance, that the school in Table 3 is performing well in the mathematics test, where it is already in the upper quartile for the group, but poorly in reading, where it is below the median for other similar schools.

Value-added information

Value-added information means that raw scores for test results have been altered to allow for the characteristics of the intake of the school, those aspects which are beyond its control, such as environmental factors and the stage of English language development.

Thomas, Sammons and Street, in their article on value-added approaches, give the following purposes of measuring the educational 'value added' contributed by a school:

> ■ *it offers a fairer and meaningful way of presenting school examination results*
>
> ■ *it is a tool which can provide both detailed and summary data that a school can analyse as part of its self-evaluation*
>
> ■ *it can be used to examine trends in value-added performance over time, in relation to school improvement initiatives*
>
> ■ *it provides performance measures that can be contrasted against other types of data available in schools such as information about the views of key groups obtained using teacher, parent and pupil questionnaires and*
>
> ■ *it can provide additional guidance in monitoring and target setting for individual pupils and specific groups of pupils (such as boys or girls or certain ethnic groups).*

(Thomas, Sammons and Street 1997)

The authors go on to say that 'the major difficulty of introducing a national framework for value-added measures is the lack of reliable standardised assessments to measure the prior attainment of pupils entering school . . . Finely differentiated and reliable attainment measures are necessary to describe accurately pupils' starting point'. This seems in conflict with the policy of accrediting a number of quite different baseline schemes, and many teachers will be wondering why a national baseline scheme has not been considered. Furthermore, as discussed in the previous section on baseline assessment, the more 'finely tuned' the assessments, the more likely they are to be time consuming and based on tight procedures, possibly marginalising observation, dialogue and questioning, all of which can be interpreted differently by teachers. Most teachers would be unhappy with a baseline assessment which was not based on these strategies, considering the age of the children.

The following section is worth reproducing from the article by Thomas *et al*, as it provides a practical example of an LEA value-added analysis in order to assist primary schools' self-evaluation, thus demonstrating the potential and usefulness of the value-added approach. It focuses on Surrey LEA, one of the few LEAs who have had baseline assessment in place for a number of years, thus enabling value-added analysis to take place for Key Stage 1 results:

6 *Surrey LEA introduced baseline reception screening for all pupils on entry in September 1993. The Year R screening comprises nine sub-scales which cover five main areas: language, early literacy, mathematics, drawing skills and social skill.*

In 1996 a multilevel analysis of pupils' 1996 KS1 results was carried out to examine:

(i) the links between pupils' reception screening results and their later performance at KS1;
(ii) impact of pupil background factors; and
(iii) provision of simple feedback for schools about the value added at KS1 after controlling for differences in pupil intake.

The findings included evidence of significant differences between schools in value-added measures. In some schools pupils were performing significantly better or worse than predicted for each KS1 outcome measure. For 28 per cent of the 107 schools involved (30 schools), reading results were significantly better or worse than predicted. For writing, 39 schools showed significantly better or worse results (36%). For mathematics the significant differences were found for 39 schools (39%) and for science the figure was 44 schools (41%). Schools also showed some important internal variations on their effectiveness. Only a small minority (seven schools) had a significantly better or worse impact on all four measures at KS1. By contrast, a quarter of the sample were performing broadly as expected in all areas. This analysis gave headteachers important feedback to raise questions about current patterns of achievement and Surrey LEA advisors have produced guidance about ways of interpreting the results. **9**

(Thomas *et al* 1997)

Summative tests

Much has been written about the impact of tests on the curriculum and teaching. We know that what is included in a test becomes the focus of teachers' teaching, because they want their children to do well. Where the test is 'high stakes', as in England and Wales, where school comparisons of results are made, teachers also 'teach to the test' or help them to pass the test by using practice papers or test-type materials (Shephard 1992, Madaus 1988). It depends on the content of the test as to whether we view these effects as positive or negative. If, for instance, the test content focuses on knowledge, skills and conceptual understanding, its impact could enhance teaching and learning. However, if the test focuses only on knowledge, we might consider that its effect would be more harmful. Therefore it is not the notion of testing which is important so much as the content of the test (Resnick and Resnick 1992). The exception to this is the current system of testing children at the end of Key Stage 1 who are either aged 6 or 7 years old. The SCAA Key Stage 1 evaluation of statutory testing in 1997, directed by

Clarke and Gipps, led us to conclude that testing for this age group will never be a truly consistent and standardised activity, because of differences of administration (e.g. different group sizes, different help and encouragement given and so on).

In previous chapters, I have challenged the notion that tests are the best vehicle for measuring and comparing achievement, but the reality for schools is that we are embedded in a test culture. Because the statutory tests are taken by every child in the country, it appears to be the best benchmark for measuring and comparing, even though the tests may not be as valid or reliable or contain as much assessment of 'deep learning' as opposed to 'shallow learning' as we would wish.

Teacher Assessment, as an equal partner to test results, provides us, at least, with the opportunity to ensure that those aspects of the curriculum not included in the test are the subject of our planning and targeting, as well as those items which appear in the tests. Research carried out by the Institute of Education for SCAA has shown on several occasions that the majority of teachers think that Teacher Assessment is more valid and reliable, and more important than standard testing (Gipps and Clarke 1998), which implies that they therefore aim for a broad and balanced curriculum in their teaching. However, the fact that teachers use a variety of different strategies for determining 'best fit' (Gipps, Clarke and McCallum 1998) means that the interpretation of levels is variable.

QCA have introduced optional tests at Year 4, followed by further optional tests for the end of Years 3 and 5. These tests could most usefully be used to support the target setting framework outlined in Chapter 4, to see whether children are 'on track', although Teacher Assessment decisions would be equally, if not more important when considering a child's progress.

Some schools buy in commercially produced tests, mainly reading tests, which they administer at the end of every year or at regular intervals, in order to, again, keep track of children's progress, ensuring that children progress steadily. However, these tests can only be used to create a graded scale, as long as the same test is used, within the context of the actual test. If the results of one test were to be compared with those of another test for the same child, the scores would be quite likely to be different, so tests are most useful in tracking progress rather than establishing actual performance.

Some schools, especially within the context of Key Stage 2, have introduced 'end of module' tests: school-based tests written by teachers to find out how much children know and what level they have achieved at the end of a unit of work which will not be repeated (e.g. a science topic). This informs teacher planning, report writing and end of Key Stage levelling.

Conclusion

Formal testing, while useful for some purposes, does not in itself appear to raise standards. Formative assessment strategies, however, can. Black and Wiliam's work showed that:

> *Innovations which include strengthening the practice of formative assessment produce significant, and often substantial, learning gains. These studies range over ages (from five year olds to university undergraduates), across several school subjects, and over several countries.*

(Black and Wiliam 1998)

While we appear to be overwhelmed by a testing and measuring regime, the way forward for actual practice appears to be to increase the expertise of formative assessment strategies in the classroom. This book will, I hope, provide teachers with an overview of the range of possibilities, the exciting potential of involving children in their own learning and the inspiration to realise the power of the teacher in focusing children's learning, providing appropriate feedback, increasing self-esteem and raising achievement for all.

References

AAIA (Association of Assessment Inspectors and Advisers) (1997) *Baseline Assessment*, AAIA Publications.

Airasian, P. (1988) 'Measurement driven instruction: a closer look', *Educational Measurement: Issues and practice*, Winter, pp. 6–11.

Barber, M. (1996) *The Learning Game*, Victor Gollancz.

Black, P. and Wiliam, D. (1998) 'Assessment and Classroom Learning', *Assessment in Education, 5*, 1.

Clarke, S. and Atkinson, S. (1996) *Tracking Significant Achievement in Primary Mathematics*, Hodder and Stoughton.

Crooks, T. J. (1988) The impact of classroom evaluation practices on students, *Review of Educational Research, 58*, 438–81.

Dearing, R. (1993) *The National Curriculum and Its Assessment: Final Report*, School Curriculum and Assessment Authority.

DFEE (1997) *From Targets to Action*, Department for Education and Employment Standards and Effectiveness Unit.

Drummond, M. J. (1993) *Assessing Children's Learning*, David Fulton Publishers.

Gipps, C. and Clarke, S. (1998) *Monitoring consistency in teacher assessment and the impact of SCAA's guidance materials at Key Stages 1, 2 and 3*, Qualifications and Curriculum Authority.

Gipps, C., Clarke, S. and McCallum, B. (1998) *The Role of the Teacher in National Assessment in England*, AERA Conference, San Diego 1998.

Harlen, W. and James, M. (1997) Assessment and learning: differences and relationships between formative and summative assessment, *Assessment in Education*.

Madaus, G. (1988) The Influence of testing on the Curriculum, in Tanner, L. (ed.), *Critical Issues in Curriculum, 87th Yearbook of NSSE Part 1*, University of Chicago Press, Chicago, Ill., pp. 83–121.

OFSTED (1996) *Framework for the Inspection of Schools*, OFSTED.

QCA (1997) *Standards Reports*.

QCA (1998) *The baseline assessment information pack*.

QCA (1998) *Assessment and Reporting Arrangements*.

Resnick, L. B. and Resnick, D. P. (1992) Assessing the thinking curriculum: New tools for educational reform, in Gifford, B. and O'Connor, M. (eds) *Changing Assessments: Alternative views of Aptitude, Achievement and Instruction*, Kluwer.

Sadler, D. (1989) Formative assessment and the design of instructional systems, *Instructional Science, 18*, 119–44.

SCAA/QCA (1994–) *Assessment and Reporting Arrangements*, School Curriculum and Assessment Authority/ Qualifications and Curriculum Authority.

SCAA (1996) *Desirable Outcomes for Children's Learning on Entering Compulsory Education*, School Curriculum and Assessment Authority.

SCAA (1997) *Teacher Assessment in Key Stage 2*, School Curriculum and Assessment Authority.

SCAA (1997) *Target Setting and Benchmarking in Schools*: consultation paper, School Curriculum and Assessment Authority.

SCAA (1997) *Looking at Children's Learning*, School Curriculum and Assessment Authority.

Schunk, D. H. (1996) Goal and self-evaluative influences during children's cognitive skill learning, *American Educational Research Journal, 33*, 359–82.

Shephard, L. (1992) *Will National Tests Improve Student Learning?* CSE Technical Report 342, CRESST, University of Colorado.

Stobart, G. and Gipps, C. (1997) *Assessment: A teachers' guide to the issues*, Hodder and Stoughton.

Surrey County Council (1997) *Year R Baseline Assessment*.

Thomas, S., Sammons, P. and Street, H. (1997) Value-added Approaches: Fairer Ways of Comparing Schools, *SIN Research Matters*, No. 7.

Tunstall, P. and Gipps, C. (1996) How does your teacher help you make your work better? Children's understanding of formative assessment, *The Curriculum Journal, 7*, 2, 185–203.

Vispoel, W. P. and Austin, J. R. (1995) Success and failure in junior high school: a critical incident approach to understanding students' attributional beliefs, *American Educational Research Journal, 32*, 2, 377–412.

White Paper (1997) *Excellence in Schools*, The Stationery Office CM 3681.

Willes, M. (1983) *Children into Pupils*, Routledge and Kegan Paul.